HOLDING PATTERNS

HOLDING PATTERNS

What to do while you're waiting…for God

Roland Boyce

On the Tracks Media

HOLDING PATTERNS
What to do while you're waiting...for God

Printed in the United States of America.

ISBN: 978-1-7369703-8-6

Cover and interior design by Rick Lindholtz for On the Tracks Media

On the Tracks Media LLC
onthetracksmedia.com

DEDICATION

I dedicate this book to my family members, teachers, pastors, colleagues, church members, and friends who have waited with me through my seasons of life. Their prayers, counsel, and encouragement helped me survive my *holding patterns*!

FORWARD

Most authors have someone else write their forward for them. But for this book, I decided to write my own.

Being on hold in life is a common denominator of being alive, of living life. We are all waiting for something all the time! I have known a variety of *holding patterns* in my seventy-plus years of life:

- In high school, waiting to be elected to office after losing the race for class president three times.
- Waiting to see if I would ever marry after the love of my life declined my proposal.
- In the early years of marriage, waiting four years for a child after we experienced a miscarriage.
- Waiting to enter the pastorate after 13 years of campus ministry.
- While pastoring, waiting several years for an opportunity to get out of a tough assignment
- I was diagnosed with Parkinson's Disease in 2000 and was anxious about its impact on my life and ministry.
- Navigating through the challenges of child-rearing in the adolescent years compounded by the pressures that pastor's children face.
- Waiting 16 years for my first book to be published.

Each holding pattern will have unique challenges, frustrations, lessons, and benefits. Though life is brief, waiting for things to happen can seem like an eternity. After all, God has an aerial view of life; we view it from the tarmac, often taxiing without taking off. Oh sure, we learn things about ourselves, life, and others after the holding pattern is over, but we're often not sure it was worth the wait...and yet before we know it, we're in another one!

Reading this book is like having a casual, easy conversation with a friend. So as you read this book, know that I am walking with you through it, discovering how men and women in Bible times faced, worked through, and learned from their *holding patterns*. Hopefully, we will learn principles and gain perspectives to help us wait out our *holding patterns* in modern times.

Roland Boyce
June 2022

TABLE OF CONTENTS

OLD TESTAMENT

The Books of the Law

Historical Books

Poetical Books

Prophetical Books

NEW TESTAMENT

Gospels

Christ's Earthly Ministry

INTRODUCTION TO HOLDING PATTERNS

(What to do while you're waiting...for God)

Ever make a call, get put on hold while you waited to be transferred to the right person and had to listen to syrupy elevator music or a host of annoying advertisements?

Sometimes the wait is a few seconds; sometimes, the wait is much longer as your call is responded to in the order in which it was received. On the long-wait days, you could wallpaper your living room. Life is like that.

It's a series of *holding patterns*, some short, some longer. There are seasons of waiting for significant things to happen; being able to conceive a child, finding the right job, or restoring a broken relationship. We wait and hope for a loved one to recover from an illness, or we grieve through their death. We wait to overcome an addiction, find a spouse, or rebuild our lives after a divorce.

The inspiration for this book originated in a counseling session with a couple waiting for employment, having children, and a potential re-location all at once! Their four-year holding pattern was intensive and depressive, like moving in slow motion through a tunnel with no light at the end.

Reality check: Everyone has been, is, or will be in a holding pattern at some point in their life. We will always be waiting for something in our earthly pilgrimage. Just as we are waiting for our phone call to be transferred, we are waiting for our call to God to be connected. We try to understand why we must wait so long for Him to answer us as we try to hold on in hope.

Millions of people have lived through the pain of a pandemic in lockdown. We've faced the fear of illness, job loss, a depressed economy, a totally reordered life of masking, and social distancing. We lived with school closures, cancellation of events, loved ones dying or giving birth alone, living with quotas on church and family gatherings, and whether to get vaccinated. Waiting thru this elongated holding pattern has been excruciating, exasperating, and beyond explanation.

Fortunately, God's Book is not filled with superheroes who lived perfect lives, had no problems, or never got frustrated when waiting for God. We don't see them as air-brushed people who always understood what He was doing, why He didn't do what they wanted or didn't do things when they wanted Him to. As a result, they lost confidence in His ability to come through for them. Instead, they were people who had doubt, fear, impatience, anger, and hopelessness when waiting for God to do something...anything!

Over 100 holding patterns in the scriptures will help you identify with those who've gone before you; what they went through, how long it took, and the result of waiting. It will allow you to apply the principles to your own life personally.

The reader will find lots of company and much encouragement from the true-to-life experiences in the lives of the Patriarchs, the nation of Israel, the prophets, and other leading biblical personalities like Jacob, Moses, Esther, Job, Daniel, Mary, and Joseph, the disciples, members of the early church, and Christ Himself!

Even reading this book constitutes a holding pattern depending on how long it takes to read it. Use it as a life laboratory workbook; absorb its truth, and apply the principles to understand and survive your own *holding patterns*.

Definition of a holding pattern:

- A predetermined maneuver that keeps the aircraft within a specified airspace while awaiting further clearance from the air traffic controller.

- A delaying tactic that completes abnormal or emergency procedures any time that a flight delay is required.

- A pilot uses a specified set of systems as a reference point in establishing and maintaining the aircraft's position while holding.

- A state or period of no progress or change.

Holding patterns will help you identify with those who have gone before us, what they went through, how long it took, and the result of waiting. It will also allow you to apply the principles to your life personally. Each holding pattern is explored from the standpoint of Background, Narrative, Principle, Perspective, and Participation, allowing the reader to reflect on and personally apply the holding pattern truth to their own situation.

THE PREMISE OF *HOLDING PATTERNS*

Holding patterns is intended to be a highly personal and practical book thru which the reader understands the normalcy of *holding patterns* throughout human history and the whole of the Holy Scriptures. Everyone has had a *holding pattern*; even the Holy Trinity has experienced this phenomenon.

Thus, people of contemporary times can identify and find themselves in the life experiences of those who have gone before them. Of course, no two people will go through the same experience or respond to it in the same way. But some similarities may help you cope with these duplicate *holding patterns*. Such identification is not to marginalize or minimize your pain or discomfort but to help you view it from a different perspective. Comparing your holding pattern to those of greater duration and intensity may help you develop greater hope and patience. Significant to these similarities of experience is the place of God's perspective, understanding of, and involvement in our holding pattern. After all, He has been with each person thru each holding pattern/waiting zone. This truth is underscored by the fact that God will be in a holding pattern until eternity; He empathizes with and enables us to get through the waiting zones and *holding patterns* of our lives!

THE PARADIGM OF *HOLDING PATTERNS*

Background: The historical background of an individual's holding pattern and their reactions to it.
Narrative: How we see the principle actualized in our contemporary world.
Principle: The particular truth we learn about each holding pattern.
Perspective: A reference that helps the reader correlate the principle with biblical truth.
Participation: The opportunity for the reader to reflect on the principle within the context of their own life.

How to use ***Holding patterns***

- Identify and mark the personalities and situations you can identify with.
- Form a Bible study or small group utilizing it as the basis of conversation and exploration.
- Use as a daily devotional reading one pattern at a time.
- **KEY** - *Holding patterns* is not a book to be read straight through, but slowly, allowing significant time to reflect

on the *Participation* section after each holding pattern, then recording your answers to the questions in a journal for further review and follow-up.

THE OLD TESTAMENT

Adam and Eve waited a lifetime to die. (Genesis 2-3)
Background: In the opening chapters of the first book of the Old Testament, we are introduced to our first parents, Adam and Eve, living in Eden, now present-day Iran. They had no parents. They were unique from us in that they were born adults. Thus, they had no in-laws, and family gatherings were uneventful until they had children, of course! Adam was alone initially. (A situation he might have wanted to return to after the fall!) God made the first wife out of Adam's rib. Her name means mother of life. The first couple was fairly typical. Adam was most likely in his man cave; Eve was ever investigative, checking out paradise and asking questions like why she and Adam were denied access to one specific tree!

Pre-flood people were vegetarians...so meal planning was easy; you pretty much nibbled fruit off the trees and plants in the ground, which initially didn't need weeding. There was lots of free time; the earth was self-watering by a mist from the ground. Apparently, Eve found the tree of the knowledge of good and evil too attractive and too hard to resist. So, Adam became a co-participant in the original sin, which altered history forever.

Satan, who was kicked out of heaven for wanting to dethrone God, came to earth. He was no longer a ruler in heaven but became the king of the earth, if only for a short season. Adam and Eve bought the line, took the bait, and ate.

They now thought they were as wise as God, but everything changed in an instant. Suddenly there were seasons; the world's climate could now be cold and wet.

The former paradise became a permanent weed patch, and childbirth would be no trip to Disneyworld. And though they didn't die immediately, as the Devil promised, they began to die a slow, gradual death. As a result, they began to show the signs of aging, something, no doubt, accelerated by raising kids.

Additionally, the overall health of humanity was affected. Thus, the first holding pattern was waiting to die; neither knew when. Adam's holding pattern was 930 years. No mention was made of Eve's longevity. The birth of children represented a second holding pattern. They had no idea how long their children would live, or how they would turn out! Little did they know that they would lose their first son at the hands of his brother early in life. God also knew that He would lose a son temporarily centuries later as He came to redeem us from the effects of sin, as forecasted in chapter two of Genesis. It records both the sin and the promise of salvation through God's Son.

Narrative: People have wrestled with three basic questions throughout history: Where do we come from? Why are we here? Where are we going? The answers are sourced in God, the Father, Son, and the Holy Spirit. God created us in His likeness to know and live for Him. We will ultimately stand before the Lord in judgment, depending on what we have believed and how we have lived our lives. These questions become more critical as we are prepared to leave this earthly life through death.

Principle: Like Adam and Eve, we're all in a holding pattern waiting to die. Many of us are also waiting for the Promised One to complete the process of salvation and give us new bodies and a new place to live.

Perspective: Psalm 90:12 "Teach us to number our days and recognize how few they are; help us to spend them as we should."
Participation: What is your outlook on life; how are you attempting to live out your days productively?

Noah waited 120 years for an ark to be built. (Genesis 6-9)
Background: When we think of this man, we almost always remember the world's largest home improvement project. (He was the Tim Allen Tool Time man of his time.) He was commissioned to build the floating zoo when he was 600 years old. This was no ordinary houseboat. It was 1.4 million cubic feet, the size of 522 railroad cars, able to house approximately 7,000 creatures in all, only using 60% of the actual space. God's patience had run out after 950 years, and He brought the world's first rainfall and flood. 270 extra-biblical accounts confirm the authenticity of this cataclysmic event. The waters that encircled the earth put the mountains under twenty-two and half feet of water for 152 days before the ark was parked on 17,000-foot-high Mt Ararat. Noah's name means rest. And indeed he did! (A mountain top experience, literally.)

Noah's obedience did not make him popular with his jeering neighbors. He was a righteous man in a sea of sinning. On the contrary, his pagan peers pressured him to give up the arduous assignment with harassment. (After all, who could get excited about living on a planet that was about the become the world's largest water park?)

God's purpose in making this super submarine out of gopher wood was to wipe the world's sinful state clean and start over by saving the only righteous family. We wonder what happened to Noah's own parents, siblings, or the new families of his three sons. (I guess that took care of conflict with the in-laws!)

The ark symbolized the salvation which would come centuries later thru Christ, who became the Savior of the world. This was alluded to in I Peter 3:18a. "Christ also suffered. He died once for the sins of all us guilty sinners although He himself was innocent of any sin at any time, that He might bring us safely home to God." (NIV) This event also commemorates giving the first five covenants, the agreements initiated and entered into by God with the human race. The Noahic Covenant guaranteed that God would never destroy the world by water; it would be dissolved by fire the next time. His promise was sealed by the first rainbow, produced by the sun shining through the rainstorm. God would also sustain them thru the four seasons, fall, winter, and spring, in what had been endless summer. (A perpetual Bahamas!) Several *holding patterns* are present here. God was waiting for His wrath to be poured out in a flood on people who had become increasingly wicked: Noah was waiting for 120 years for the project to be completed amid great harassment. Finally, Noah and his family were waiting for the water to recede, no doubt wondering what shape their world would be in. (Surprise!)

Narrative: When we enter the relationships of marriage, parenting, or the work arena, we don't know the duration of those earthly assignments. Yet, we are required to be steadfast in carrying them out. If we knew ahead of time what it would take, we might sign off on them before they even got started.

Principle: *Holding patterns* sometimes require us to remain steadfast in our assigned task without knowing how long it will take to complete it.
Perspective: Philippians 1:6 "And I am sure that God who began the good work within you will keep right on helping you

grow in His grace until His task within you is finally finished on that day when Jesus Christ returns."
Participation: Re-call an assignment when you needed to be steadfast. Why was it hard, and how did you feel when it ended?

Abraham waited 86 years to be a father. (Genesis12-15)
Background: *The birth of a nation.* Abraham moved his family from the Ur of the Chaldees to Cannan when he was 75. Imagine being outdoors on a clear night, seeing the stars in their vast array, and having God speak to you out of the blue. It was logical to use the stars and the sand metaphor to describe how many offspring Abraham would have. The forecast would require the work of the impossibility specialist to do what Abraham and Sarah could not do on their own; conceive a child. Pretty hard to be the father of nations when you aren't a father! Yet Abram, exalted father, became Abraham, father of many nations, based on a Covenant which bore his name. From his offspring came the three great world religions, Judaism, Christianity, and Muslim.

Abraham had a good life apart from parenthood. He was a well-to-do merchant with huge herds and personal servants. He could have bought anything he wanted, except a child. He was a man who learned to wait. At the age of 100, he became the father of Isaac. The name God gave Abraham was emblematic of his circumstances. El Elyon means the Sovereign Lord who made a covenant with him and gave him an unconditional legacy.

The birth of a child. **Living a lifetime of fear of what Ishmael would become and how he would treat Isaac's descendants**. (Genesis 16-18) Mr. and Mrs. Abraham weren't sure their God could pull off plan A, so they impatiently put plan B in place.

Sarah encouraged Abraham to conceive a child thru her handmaiden, Hagar. She bore him a son, Ishmael. God blessed him, but God still intended to fulfill His Covenant with them thru Isaac. (God may have said, “Thanks for your help, but I’m doing it my way and going with plan A.”) Three angelic messengers delivered the divine birth announcement to the prospective father and mother.

Their child was born and named Isaac, which means laughter. This described the disbelief and joy of his parents when they heard the forecast. But let's not be too hard on them. Here is a 90-year-old woman who probably pondered the impossibility of a sexual relationship with her fossil husband, the pain of a worn-out uterus, and birth without an epidural. Who wouldn't have laughed; cried would be more like it! They had waited almost a century for this moment. Nevertheless, God still made good on His promise to bless Ishmael, the Wild One, descriptive of his temperament and posterity. His 12 sons founded today's modern Arab kingdom, and his descendants became Israel's arch enemy.

The sacrifice of a child. **Experiencing a brief but intensive waiting zone before taking his son's life.** (Genesis 22)
One of the shortest *holding patterns* centered in God's request/mandate to Abraham is to offer his son, Isaac, a living sacrifice. Isaac wasn’t a young boy. Historians speculate he was at least a young adult. God asked for Abraham’s son, conceived by miraculous conception, to be given back to Him. He was asking Abraham, who loved his son, Isaac, to give him up as a living sacrifice which would mean that he would be slain in place of an animal sacrifice.

Imagine the overwhelming fear, confusion, anger, and grief that gripped the heart of this aged father who had waited so long for the son he was about to give up, and also the vision of being the father of many nations. The father grieved for his son's potential death in the agonizing hours that preceded it, painful beyond description. Yet, this act of faith and obedience became a forerunner to the death of another son. Centuries later, the living Lamb of God who was slain for the world's sins.

Narrative: Sometimes, it is a toss-up as to which holding pattern is more stressful, a long or a short one. The long one can be compared to when someone suffers for an extended period before dying. The short one can be compared to when a person dies suddenly, and their family has no time to prepare for and adjust to it. The benefit of a short holding pattern, though intensive, is that it ends quickly. The longer ones may be more painful. Instead, Abraham experienced both in his life. Someday it will be interesting to ask him which one he preferred!

Principle: The pain of the shorter holding pattern can be more concentrated and pass more quickly.
Perspective: Hebrews 10:35-36 "Do not let this happy trust in the Lord die away, no matter what happens. Remember your reward! You need to keep on patiently doing God's will if you want Him to do for you all that He has promised."
Participation: Identify a short holding pattern in your life that was very intensive but passed quickly. Why was it intensive?

Jacob and Rachel waited 14 years to marry each other. (Genesis 29:14-28)
Background: Jacob was out to find a wife, no doubt a lot like his mother, Rebekah. She sent him to her brother, Uncle Laban, who had two daughters. Leah was the plain one; Rachael could have modeled for the Canaanite Chronicle. Jacob promises to work seven years for Rachael. But the guy

who deceived his own dad, Isaac, was now deceived by his mother's brother. (Must have been in the family DNA.)

The sneaky uncle switched daughters on the wedding night, and Jacob wound up with Leah. (He apparently did not get a good look at the bride in the dark tent!) A wee bit agitated, the forlorn groom promised to work seven more years for Rachael. Poor Jacob. After being married to the wrong one for seven years, how would you like to wait for the right one for 14 years?

Narrative: At one time or another, we have all been promised something by someone who didn't follow through. The classic example is a parent promising to do something for or with their child who forgets or never intends to do it. This often affects the child for the rest of their life, producing mistrust and feelings of worthlessness due to invalidation.

Principle: *Holding patterns* can be frustrating when you are waiting for someone to do what they promised.
Perspective: Joshua 21:45 “Every good thing the Lord had promised them came true.”
Participation: Many of us have had to go through life regretting that someone who promised us something didn't come through. Did this ever happen to you? What feelings did you have? How have you handled those feelings? What if you were the one who didn’t come through; then what?

Jacob and Esau did not see each other for over 20 years and were unsure if they would live through the reunion. (Genesis 25-33)

Background: After 20 years of barrenness, God granted the prayer of Isaac and allowed Rebekah to conceive, the result of which was a double blessing of twins, Abraham's grandsons, born in approximately BC 2005.

Isaac was 60 when they were born. (I mean, raising twins is one thing when you're the age of most new parents, but having teenagers in your eighties is quite another!) Raising them was compounded by Isaac's preference for Esau, the outdoorsman; their mother's favorite was Jacob, the domestic type.

So as Isaac was preparing to die, it came time for the blessing. Rebekah tried to pull a fast one on her ailing husband by disguising Jacob to look, sound, and even smell like his older brother to get his father's blessing before he died. Although the father was suspicious, it worked, and he blessed Jacob first. Only after Esau came to him for the blessing did he realize what had happened; he was mortified, and Esau was livid. After all, Jacob's name means deceiver. Esau held a grudge against his brother (I'll bet!) and plotted to kill him. Remember, however, that Esau had sold his birthright for a happy meal, so now it was alright for the blessing to go to the wrong twin! The brothers were separated for the next 21 years covering five chapters of Genesis, enough for Jacob to father nine more children. Finally, in chapter 33, the brothers were reunited amicably.

Two *holding patterns* present themselves in these four lives. First, Isaac and Rebekah waited for twenty years for their boys. Then, the boys don't see each other for almost a quarter of a century. Apparently, absence in this situation did not make the heart grow fonder!

Narrative: You or I have likely been at odds with someone we love, often a family member. We have memories of ruined holidays, people not speaking to each other for long periods, and relatives not forgiving someone who offended them. Some die without resolving interpersonal issues. Jacob and Esau were the poster children of this dysfunctional phenomenon. They did not see or speak to each other after boyhood, living with anger, hate, and resentment that ate at them. They lived in fear of what the other brother would do. Yet, desperation and emotional exhaustion finally drove them to reconcile and end the stand-off.

Principle: Many of us have had intensified *holding patterns* due to strained relationships with family members.

Perspective: Romans 12:19 "Dear friends, never avenge yourselves. Leave that to God, for He has said that He will repay those who deserve it. Don't take the law into your own hands."

Participation: Give an instance when you took the initiative to restore a relationship with someone close to you or someone who took that initiative with you. What was the outcome? If there was no closure, how have you lived with the situation?

Joseph was in prison for two years on false charges. (Genesis 39-40)

Background: God was with the kidnap victim. Joseph, who made friends and influenced people, quickly got an entry-level position. He served as the household manager at the home of one of Pharaoh's officials, Potiphar. But his first job became complicated by Mrs. Potiphar, who had a fatal attraction to the handsome Hebrew and accused him of adultery.

After the plan failed, the spurned lover cried foul and got her household CEO tossed into prison. He was befriended by two other cellmates put there by Pharaoh to be punished by death. They both had dreams which only the vision expert could translate. One of the men would be released; one would die just as was predicted. The one who lived promised to put in a good word for him to the Egyptian officials; he promptly forgot to do it. Joseph remained in prison until the Pharaoh asked him to interpret his dream.

They would have never seen each other again, except God had already planned to use Joesph to tell Pharaoh what his dream meant. But unfortunately, it translated into a real-life disaster that gripped Egypt for seven years, affecting a vast region, including Joseph's homeland of Canaan. Unbeknown to his family, he had been promoted from household manager to Vice-President of the country and head of the Department of Agriculture. His job was to stockpile grain for seven good years to prepare for the coming famine when buying a loaf of bread would be difficult. On top of being kidnapped, left for dead, and exported to a foreign land, God used Joseph to save two nations, Egypt and Israel.

Narrative: We would be considered weird if we asked God for opportunities to grow thru adversity, especially when it comes from people who are supposed to love us! It's like asking God for patience by giving us more difficulty. Life gives us enough of those situations without our asking for them, right? So we don't have to ask for adversity; it has a way of finding us anyway!

Principle: *Holding patterns* can provide the opportunity to build perseverance in the face of opposition.
Perspective: James 1:4 "So let it grow, and don't try to squirm out of your problems. For when your patience is finally in full bloom, then you will be ready for anything, strong in character, full and complete."

Participation: How has struggling with a problematic situation strengthened your faith, or has it?

Joseph went without seeing his family for 25 years. (Genesis 37-39, 42-50)

Background: Joseph, whose name means God will add, was one of the two sons of Jacob and long-baren Rachel; he was one of a kind. Maybe being his parent's favorite made him spoiled and obnoxious, especially to his 11 other brothers. Oneiromancy is the science of interpreting dreams; he had the dream gene, just like Daniel.

So, he kept having these weird dreams about bunches of grain and the sun, moon, and stars bowing down to him. And these bedtime stories made his brothers hate him.

In fact, they hated him so much that they pretended to kill him; but actually sold him as a slave to a caravan of merchants going to Egypt! His deportation at the hand of angry, jealous brothers resulted in an estrangement from the family, which became the narrative for the rest of Genesis.

Joseph's brothers fabricated the story of his death to their father using his cloak of many colors dipped in the blood of a slaughtered animal. They didn't know where he wound up, as if they cared. (At least no more boring bedtime stories!)

This scenario set the stage for one of the most monumental and memorable family reunions in human history. Jacob sent his sons to Egypt to buy grain from the last person on earth they expected to find handing it out. In chapter 46, Jacob, now Israel, joined his sons to see his long-lost son, whom he presumed dead. Joseph welcomed and cared for them, especially his younger brother, Benjamin, Rachel's only other son.

Joseph held no grudges but instead explained to his brothers that what they intended for evil turned out to be something good, saving their lives from famine. Their attempt at endangering his life resulted in his ability to save theirs. Joseph, like Isaac, became a symbol of the Savior who would thru tragedy, save people from their disaster. Jacob had to wait a significant length of time before seeing him alive, grown, and the father of two sons of his own. Joseph's brothers lived thru the same holding pattern, plagued by the guilt of what they had done and the potential ramifications of their misdeeds.

Joseph waited in a 25-year holding pattern. He was unsure he'd ever see his family alive again. Finally, this happened in Egypt when disbelief became a jubilant celebration. It was one definitely worth waiting for! But in the most challenging years of his life in a strange land with a huge task, he was cut off from the very people he needed most.

Narrative: Ever feel like everyone has deserted you and left you alone to face your crisis? A spouse, your children, someone you confided in, or a close friend who wanted nothing to do with you when you told them the truth?

Principle: *Holding patterns* are intensified when you have to go through them alone.
Perspective: Psalm 27:10 "For if my father and mother should abandon me, you would welcome and comfort me."
Participation: Were you ever separated from your family? How did that affect you; affect them? If yet estranged, how have you chosen to live with this issue?

Moses waited 40 years to lead Israel out of Egypt. (Exodus 2)

Background: After the passing of Joseph, in the 15th century BC, another Pharaoh came to power who didn't know Joseph from Adam or his people and missed the history lesson on famines! The group of 70 had become a nation of 6,000,000 people; allies had become enemies. Now threatened by Joseph's decedents, this Pharaoh had the gruesome idea to circumvent the population explosion. Kill all the boy babies!

Moses was a boy child, and his mother, Jochebed, could not think of throwing him into the river. Instead, she had a counter-idea; put the baby in a basket that could float on top of the river. So she instructed her daughter Miriam to place the 'Moses basket' in the Nile River, hoping he would be discovered. Not by accident, but by divine design, the daughter of Pharaoh just *happened* to be walking by the river at the exact time the baby cried. Her maternal instincts went into overdrive, and she adopted him on the spot. (Without any social workers and reams of paperwork!) Apparently, her dad, the Pharoah, didn't care that she had a Hebrew son or was too busy building pyramids to check! Raised in the Egyptian public school system, he knew several languages, excelled in archery and horseback riding. This Jewish child raised in Egypt became a significant player on the Old Testament world stage.

Narrative: Exasperation probably describes how we have felt when some project or undertaking was moving way too slowly. We seemingly had no way to get it off the tarmac: Renovating the kitchen, getting your Master's, not being proposed to after eight years of courtship, or saving enough money to travel to Jamaica. Our mantra is to forget patience, build character, and cultivate virtue; let's get this show on the road!

Principle: Our entire life is a series of preparations for the upcoming *holding patterns*.
Perspective: Galatians 6:9 "And let us not get tired of doing what is right, for after a while we will reap a harvest of blessing if we don't get discouraged and give up."
Participation: What causes you to be impatient going through a holding pattern?

Moses waited for 40 years to be confronted by Egyptian rulers. (Exodus 7)
Background: Exodus also records the account of Moses confronting his former family members who charged him with manslaughter. Then he traveled home to the land of Midian, where he, the former Prince of Egypt became an ordinary sheepherder. However, he is sent there for a more important reason, to prepare for the task of herding his people out of Egypt, where they had become slaves. History records that Moses entered into a 40-year holding pattern.

Moses left Egypt at 40, a prince, and returned four decades later, at age 80, as a herdsman. He was a different man in many ways, clearly on the other side of the law. The favored son had become a righteous renegade.

I wonder if he ever missed Egypt and all the amenities of the good life. The New Testament book of Hebrews records that he preferred being mistreated rather than enjoying sin's pleasures for a season. Forty years in the scriptures is known as a generation. During this time, the oppression of his people intensified to the point of an urgently needed intervention. God was preparing Moses to be a deliverer of His people. Moses would learn to know and depend upon God in new ways. He would become known as a friend of God, the mighty deliverer, and the worker of miracles. There is a saying, "It takes 100 days to grow a squash, but 100 years to grow an oak." God obviously wanted Moses to be the oak.

Narrative: Sometimes, we want to go back to an earlier time in life when things were easier. We can get stuck in the past, unable to cope with the present or face the future. The truth is that the past will never be exactly how it was or most likely not as wonderful as we remember it. (Like going back to our hometown after 25 years.) Often, we can't change the past. It may be better to make a new situation rather than re-make an old one. We need a reset and a new start in the present.

Principle: *Holding patterns* can involve leaving behind a life that we wish we could return to, but they can also help us learn that endings can create the possibility of new beginnings.
Perspective: Philippians 3:13-14 "No, dear brothers, I am still not all I should be, but I am bringing all my energies to bear on this one thing: Forgetting the past and looking forward to what lies ahead, I strain to reach the end of the race and receive the prize for which God is calling us up to heaven because of what Christ Jesus did for us."
Participation: Is there something in your past you want to relive? If so, does it keep you from moving into the future?

Moses held his arms up for one entire day in order to conquer the enemy. (Exodus 17) *Overcoming the enemy.*
Background: Those pesky Amalekites were at it again with Israel. God had a weird strategy for conquering them. Scud missiles? Drones? Nope! Try Moses standing on the top of a hill with his hands up. (What you usually do when someone is trying to rob you!) The problem was that Moses's arms got tired, and he needed Aaron and Hur to hold them up. As long as he held them up, Israel prevailed over the Amalekites. The

length of time to execute this adroit military procedure was approximately 24 hours. What makes it unique from the others is that two other people have been involved in it. Aaron and Hur, no doubt, were waiting to take turns, changing arms, shifting positions, and wondering how long it would take to whip the opposition! (Are we there yet?)

Narrative: Many of us have thought we could go it alone, only to discover that we don't do life solo. Yet, we feel embarrassed or tentative about looking weak or incapable by seeking assistance. But, in time, we learn that it is a sign of strength, not weakness, to rely on and team up with others to survive and even thrive!

Principle: When we are on hold, we often need others to hold on with us.
Perspective: Galatians 6:2 "Share each other's troubles and problems and so obey our Lord's command."
Participation: Name two people who helped you through a holding pattern; if they are alive, thank them. If not, thank God for them. Is there someone going through a holding pattern you could help?

Moses lived the rest of his life knowing he would not enter the Promised Land. (Numbers 20) *The Water Test.*
Background: The most difficult holding pattern in Moses's life wasn't in the courts of Pharaoh or the pastures of Midian; it was after he lost his temper at the base of a rock.

The first rock incident in Exodus 17 was no problem. Moses did exactly what God told him to do. But in the second incident, Moses departed from the divine game plan; instead of speaking to the rock as God had instructed, he struck it twice, presumably in anger over the people's complaining and quarreling. (I mean, 6,000,000 people bad-mouthing God and their leaders could make you cranky, right?) It appeared that he had performed the miracle by his own power. God was not pleased with this well-meaning, exhausted, frustrated, but disobedient patriarch. As a result, he could not enter Canaan with the very people who made him mad and kept him from going in.

Moses spent the rest of his life preparing to die without entering the Promised Land. Yet, at 120 years, his eyes were not weak or his strength gone. In other words, it was a premature death; it shouldn't have been his time. Moses's hitting the rock episode illustrates this truth. Even though he didn't make the same mistake of losing his temper again, he paid dearly for the first one. (It makes me glad God doesn't deal with our anger in the same way He did in those days!)

Narrative: It is not an unusual human phenomenon to make a mistake. After all, there are no perfect people. It is natural to make mistakes, but the greater error is to repeat the past rather than learn from it. Insanity has been defined as doing the same thing repeatedly and expecting different results.

Principle: Some of us could be in *holding patterns* caused by mistakes we have made.
Perspective: Proverbs 23:12 "Don't refuse to accept criticism, get all the help you can."
Participation: What mistake taught you the most? Did you ever repeat it? What would you advise others to do in this situation?

Historical Books

The Children of Israel lived through seven sin/salvation cycles and a 70-year captivity.

Background: Upon the death of the Patriarchs, Israel was ruled by judges who guided them by God's direction and protected them from their enemies. These enemies forced Israel into *holding patterns* of a different duration, during which godless nations threatened their national security and severely disrupted their daily lives. There are seven such patterns recorded in the Old Testament.

Jebusites	Judge	Othniel
Edomites	Judge	Ehud
Canaanites	Judge	Deborah/Barak
Midianites	Judge	Gideon
Philistines	Judge	Tola
Ammonites	Judge	Jephthah
Philistines	Judge	Samson

While the judges ruled, Israel behaved itself. However, they reverted to their old behaviors once the judge died. Psalm 78 vividly describes the cycles: (Sin/Cry out/Be Delivered/Sin again.)

Their failure to follow after God and fulfill their divine purpose ultimately resulted in their 70-year-long holding pattern in captivity; Israel in Assyria and Judah in Babylon. (And a bad case of spiritual homesickness.)

We ask ourselves, why didn't they learn from their adverse experiences and stop doing the wrong things that got them in trouble repeatedly? Indeed, life under the dominion of a foreign power was challenging. It kept them from becoming the individual nation they were called to be; it caused their spiritual and national identity to be obscured. Like disobedient children who either thought they wouldn't get caught or forgot the discomfort of God's discipline, they frustrated and caused Him to be angry with them although He still loved them. They never really learned their lesson but instead did what was right in their own eyes, as recorded in the book of Judges twice.

History records that their land was ultimately taken from them and their people scattered across the face of the earth, a high price for being hard-headed and hard-hearted. The narrative of Judges helps us understand that *holding patterns* result from what we do, i.e., when we disobey and go our own way or do what is right and go God's way. God never forces us to choose.

Narrative: Which of us as parents haven't become frustrated with our children who don't listen to us and keep disobeying what we tell them? Then, when they mess up, they find a way of blaming us for being unreasonable! Well, as supposedly grown-up children, we act the same way. First, we fail to listen and obey and then blame God for the holding pattern we have created for ourselves. And by the way, now we know how God, our heavenly father, feels; frustrated!

Principle: *Holding patterns* are often the result of self-caused consequences.
Perspective: Galatians 6:7-8 "Don't be misled; remember that you can't ignore God and get away with it; a man will always reap just the kind of crop he sows! If he sows to please his own wrong desires, he will be planting seeds of evil, and he will surely reap a harvest of spiritual decay and death; but if he plants the good things of the Spirit, he will reap the everlasting life that the Holy Spirit gives him."
Participation: Identify an example of disobedience in your life. Identify the outcomes. Explain how you've become different through this experience.

Rahab waited for ten days for the destruction of Jericho to see if she and her family would be saved. (Joshua 2)
Background: We don't usually put this woman up there with the Queen of Sheba, Mary, the mother of Jesus, or Mother Theresa! (The woman was a streetwalker.) But she wound up in the Old Testament narrative and eventually in the New Testament book of Hebrews Hall of Faith. (Whoa!)

Here's the storyline: Joshua has taken over for the recently departed Moses and is on the verge of taking the land, which God had commanded the people of Israel to do. But they had to spy it out first. The venture went well because a harlot living in Jericho decided to help the spies. She heard of what God had done in judging pagan people and was scared of what He might do to her, much less her people.

God's reputation preceded him, and she was very impressed. So she helped the spies escape by hiding them under flax bales to carry out the get-away plan. The spies promised to reward her by saving her life. Fair exchange: They saved each other. Thus, she came under God's pledge of safety as visualized by a red cord on the window of her house.

But this prostitute became a God-believer; she was saved in more ways than one! She proved that God is a God of second chances who allows for u-turns on the road of life. This also caused her to change her occupation. She became the wife of Salmon, presumed to be Caleb's son. She was a leading lady in Israel, an ancestor of Boaz, and the great-great-grandmother of David from whose lineage Christ came.

So this infamous-turned-famous woman of the night became a daughter of the Light. She was in a holding pattern even though it was only ten days. It took three days for the spies to get home and seven more days for Joshua and the people of Israel to shout the walls down.

One question ran thru her mind: How long will it be until they come to rescue me? Will it be soon enough not to be found out by the city officials? But she believed in this foreign God who saved her life and her whole family and allowed her to become part of David's royal family. (Amazing grace!)

Narrative: One of the essential things in a holding pattern is to have a person or group of people help us work our way through it; losing a child prematurely, unexpected unemployment, or a divorce. No matter the potential outcome, we need someone else's strength to provide the support and encouragement we sometimes can't find within ourselves at a critical point in life.

Principle: While we wait, we need reassurance that things will turn out alright.
Perspective: Proverbs 17:17 "A true friend is always loyal, and a brother is born to help in time of need."
Participation: Identify someone who did something that encouraged you when you were waiting for an outcome. What was it?

Ruth waited an extended season to be remarried. (Ruth 2)
Background: In approximately BC 1011-971, we meet Ruth, whose name means friendship. The book's opening verses bear her name; the only other book named after a woman was the book of Esther.

Both women have something in common; they were in the right place at the right time. Both have sad stories with happy endings after being in a holding pattern. Her book is noted in biblical literature as what Venus is to sculpture and what Mona Lisa is to painting.

Here's the story: Naomi, her mother-in-law, married Elimelech. She had two sons with him, Chilon and Mahlon. (Not everyone liked simple names, like David). After her husband died, her sons married Orpah and Ruth. Then, after being married for only ten years, both sons died. Suddenly all three women were widowed. Ruth joined her mother-in-law in Bethlehem, where she was considered a foreigner and looked down on by the Moabites. Here she worked as a maidservant and eventually married a man God had already selected for her. He rewarded her obedience and faithfulness.

A holding pattern was the time between when Ruth's husband died before she would re-marry. Ruth and Boaz subsequently married and became parents of Obed, father of Jesse, who was the father of King David, a forerunner to Christ, born in the little town of Bethlehem. A grieving mother's holding pattern resulted in her obedient daughter-in-law becoming the great-grandmother of a king!

Narrative: The loss of a spouse leaves a huge vacancy that nothing can fill. Whether by divorce or death, there is agony in waiting, acute loneliness and feeling of desperation, and desertion, all of which can become part of a life lived alone.

Principle: Long seasons of devastation accompany the loss of a spouse, which can end in remarriage or remaining single.
Perspective: II Corinthians 1:6-7 "We are in deep trouble for bringing you God's comfort and salvation. But in our trouble, God has comforted us and this, too, to help you: to show you from our personal experience how God will tenderly comfort you when you undergo these same sufferings. He will give you the strength to endure."

Participation: Have you or someone you know lost a spouse prematurely? How could you help someone who has had this experience? If so, consider forming a support group to help those who have gone through it.

Hannah lived childless for a long season, then gave up her child for a lifetime of service in the Temple. (I Samuel 1-2)
Background: Hannah, whose name means grace, was one of the two wives of Elkanah. In the Old Testament, men could practice polygamy and have more than one wife. (An early version of Sister Wives?)

Elkanah has two wives, one named Peninnah and the other named Hannah. The first wife had sons and daughters. This caused great anguish for Hannah, who watched her husband bestow all kinds of favors on his other wife and her children. (This required real grace!) Adding insult to injury, Peninnah made fun of Hannah's inability to have children. The actual word used is provoked. She grieved over being unloved by her husband. (Like it was *her* fault). The more disconcerting factor was that the Lord had shut up her womb much like Sarah's. Hannah was a good and God-fearing woman who couldn't understand why God would do this to her and pleaded with Him to give her a baby. In her attempt to get what she requested, she finally promised that if the Lord gave her a child, she would give it back to Him for His service. This was a huge compromise for a first-time mother-to-be!

The Lord granted her petition by giving her a son whom she named Samuel, whose name means 'I asked of the Lord, or God hears.' He became the first prophet/priest of Israel, a man of great renown and influence, with two Old Testament books named after him. (I and II Samuel). Hannah had not one but three *holding patterns* in her life, each involving a child. Her first one was waiting to catch up with her competitor, Peninnah. It might have seemed like a short time chronologically, but it was an amazingly long and painful waiting zone for a childless woman who was not favored by her husband and ridiculed by his other wife.

The second one was the time between Samuel's birth and weaning. Although the biblical account does not give the exact period of time, Old Testament tradition indicates that the normal weaning of the child was about three years. Thirdly, Hannah knew that to fulfill her promise to God she would have to give the boy to His service permanently, although she would see him once a year at the time of Passover. (So she weaned him s-l-o-w-l-y.) Finally, she counted and treasured every day before he had to leave her.

Hannah was in the company of many other women throughout the annals of history who have not been able to bear children, some of them permanently, others who have waited an extended amount of time to hold a newborn in their arms. By the way, God not only answered her prayer once...but five more times with three sons and two daughters!

Narrative: Women are given an innate instinct to produce offspring, something most men can't and maybe don't want to understand. Insecurity, rejection, and anger can be produced by the inability to become a mother. Marriages have ended over sterility and the inability to produce offspring. Waiting for a child in any woman's life is excruciating. Although adoption and inheriting stepchildren are options, there is still something about birthing the child who becomes part of you that is unexplainable.

Principle: When we are willing to give up what we want, God will answer our request in other ways, on His terms, and within His timeline.
Perspective: I Samuel 1:8,10 "What's the matter, Hannah?" "Why aren't you eating? Why make such a fuss over having no children? Isn't having me better than having ten sons? She was in deep anguish and was crying bitterly as she prayed to the Lord."
Participation: Do you know of someone who was childless for a long time or permanently? Perhaps it was you. How did faith help you or another person through this experience?

Michal, the first wife of David, lived her whole life knowing she would never have children. (II Samuel 6:20-23)
Background: The theme of Michal's story also has to do with children; in this case, self-caused childlessness is a tragedy nonetheless. It is a strange story. Saul's daughter, Michal, was the first of David's several wives. The story begins on the *National Return of the Ark Day* in Israel. The sacred artifact had been held hostage by nasty Philistines, home of the giants. It had finally been re-captured. It was party time in Israel, and the king knew how to party hearty! He really got into it; he even danced, something not uncommon when God's Old Testament people worshipped. But apparently, his wife thought he got into it a little too much. She was embarrassed for him, for the country, for herself. She despised him for leading the homecoming parade in a Speedo.

The king felt passionate about worshiping His God, whose Old Testament dwelling place had been stolen but now returned. He was enthusiastic about praising God for its deliverance. God didn't penalize him for dancing up a storm in a loincloth. Instead, God penalized her by making her barren for the rest of her life. Her grief was compounded because she unintentionally brought this condition on herself. God honored David for his worship and dishonored Michal for her faulting him. Think of it; Michal's holding pattern spanned her entire life. She was undoubtedly tormented seeing David's other wives bearing children and subsequently becoming grandmothers; she experienced neither. However, she did adopt her sister's four children.

Narrative: Being sorry for a mistake doesn't necessarily mean we don't have to face the consequence of our choice. Frankly, it might be less painful to be in a holding pattern if it was one we did not create.

Principle: *Holding patterns* can sometimes last a lifetime, resulting in irreversible consequences.

Perspective: Psalm 103:12-13 "He has removed our sins as far away from us as the east is from the west. He is like a father to us, tender and sympathetic to those who reverence Him."

Participation: Are you living with the consequence of something you or someone you love has done? Are you able to extend or accept forgiveness to yourself or offer it to them? Are you able to move forward in your life regardless?

David waited to escape Saul. (I Samuel 19-27)

Background: The youngest of seven brothers to succeed Saul, David was a shepherd, musician, and downright handy with a sling-shot. One of the longest *holding patterns* in the Old Testament was when the king-to-be was on the run from the king; Saul was chasing David. A precursor to this fugitive-like pursuit was David taking out Goliath, becoming the royal court harpist, and establishing a close bond with Saul's son,

Jonathan. He was also heralded by the people as killing more enemies than Saul.
We don't know the actual length of this holding pattern. It was a human chess match with both kings trying to checkmate each other. (And there were no queens to help, apparently.)

The divergent outcomes for the two rulers are even more interesting than the holding pattern itself; one died, one lived. David had a couple of chances to fight fire with fire, but instead, he used water. (His men entered Saul's territory to get water for David, which he refused to drink because they risked their lives.) Thus, he spared the life of his predator. Saul eventually took his own life at the hand of his chief sword-bearer along with his three sons. Though Saul was dead, David was not allowed to rule the whole nation for another seven years. Grief! Plenty of governmental bureaucracy then too!

Narrative: We live in a Drive-thru, Easy Button culture. We are always in a hurry and don't like to wait; having what we want, how we want it, and when we want it!

Principle: What we dream and hope for does not always become a reality right away. We have to wait. We can become impatient and hopeless.
Perspective: Romans 8:19 "For all creation is waiting patiently and hopefully for that future day when God will resurrect His children."
Participation: Have you had a dream that took a long time to actualize? If it was realized, was it hard to wait? Then, finally, when it is realized, was it worth the wait? Write this principle down and put it in a prominent place!

David waited for seven days to see if his newborn son would live. (II Samuel 12:15-24)

Background: The King is now in his first holding pattern, unlike the one created by Saul; he created this one himself in the aftermath of his dual sins of adultery and murder. (Imagine!) The man, after God's own heart, was about to have his heart broken. The child conceived thru his affair with Bathsheba was going to die, possibly struck down by the Lord as compensation for the idle king's one-night stand. The new parents greatly grieved over a son's death and the sin that precipitated it. Thus, the head of state who had compromised his integrity faced outliving his offspring and the agonizing wait for his son's inevitable death.

This first holding pattern lasts a brief seven days, an eternity for the parents. Longevity was offset by intensity. But unlike other *holding patterns*, it had a happy ending. Sorrow turned into dancing when they welcomed several sons into the world, one named Solomon, his father's successor. God had fully intended to forgive the transgression after allowing them to endure the pain of their joint failure.

Narrative: *Holding patterns* are not our favorite things no matter what good comes from them. They are inevitable, but how we respond to them isn't. We often try to avoid unpleasant things. They bring us pain, but they are often the very things that help us work through it.

Principle: Longer *holding patterns* make us appreciate shorter ones. Both can produce patience and endurance.

Perspective: Romans 5:3-4 "We can rejoice, too, when we run into problems and trials, for we know that they are good for us, they help us learn to be patient. And patience develops strength of character in us and helps us trust God more each time we use it until finally our hope and faith are strong and steady."

Participation: If you have had a holding pattern involving a child, how did you make it through? Did someone you know endure this pattern? Could you help others make it through based on what you have experienced?

David experienced an intensive three-day wait while a plague killed 70,000 of his people. (II Samuel 24)

Background: People of power in high places often get carried away with their own importance, governed by elephant-sized egos. Such was the case of King David after he waited in a holding pattern for seven years to be king over both Israel and Judah. Of course, he had nothing to do but wait. But the following holding pattern, although shorter, was much more intensive. King David apparently forgot the lesson he learned from his predecessor.

He got this zany idea to number the people, particularly the military, maybe because he wanted to flex his political muscle to intimidate his neighboring nations. His cabinet appealed to their President not to do it, but he went ahead full steam with a national census despite the warning. (Hey, Presidents always listen to their advisors, right?) Forget the fact that the Hebrew Census Bureau tallied up the troops at 300,000. God was not impressed and more than a little upset with David for trusting his own strength rather than His! So there was a penalty for the nonsense census; seven years of famine, three months of David fleeing before his enemies, or three days of pestilence in the land.

David's holding pattern was nine months and 23 days. Nine months and 20 days to complete the census and three days for God to punish the king for taking it in the first place!

Undoubtedly, David experienced two different but related emotions during the almost ten months of waiting; guilt over knowing he had made a wrong choice and dreading the potential consequences of pain and death of his own people, i.e., 70,000 enlisted men! And can we imagine the intensity of waiting for the people those three l-o-n-g days, wondering if they or someone they knew would die all because the guy at the top misused his power motivated by a desire to look good?

Narrative: Much of what we deal with in life has to do with the choices others make but affects us nonetheless. A teenage mother gives up her baby for adoption. The gambler impoverishes their family. The innocent person is sent to prison. Recovering from these consequences may take a lifetime; the wound sometimes never heals.

Principle: Some *holding patterns* result from choices made by others over which we have no control.
Perspective: Matthew 2:18 "Screams of anguish come from Ramah, weeping unrestrained; Rachel weeping for her children, uncomforted for they are dead." (Herod had murdered the male children.)
Participation: Has a period of waiting in your life resulted from a choice someone else made for you? Do you have unresolved feelings about that choice? Have you been able to trust God to help you forgive that person and be released from its burden?

Solomon waited 20 years to complete two significant projects. (I Kings 6:38-7:1)
Background: David and Bathsheba's son, Solomon, was extraordinarily handsome and intelligent. (No surprise!) After beating out his fierce competitor, Adonijah, and four others for the throne, Solomon ascended to the throne of his father, David. He became one of Israel's three most renowned kings and assuredly the wisest, at least for a while. This was because when the Lord asked him what he wanted, he turned down the usual top three choices: long life, riches, or defeat of enemies. Solomon chose *wisdom* instead, which explains the intelligent part. He was a botanist, songwriter, and author of psalms and proverbs.

Solomon was renowned because God told him to build the Temple instead of his father, David. He then entered two long *holding patterns*, which involved building projects. The first was building the Temple. Construction time; seven years. The second was building his own house. Construction time; 14 years. (Twice as long). I am always amazed at the architectural acumen of people in ancient times, and how exceptionally long their buildings lasted. (The Temple would have lasted longer if the Romans hadn't destroyed it.)

So about now, you're asking, did God really need a place to live? After all, He has the whole world. And it says that God would not dwell in a house made by human hands. But, He commanded it to be a place where He could reside with His people for worship. Sadly, Solomon's multiple wives led him to idolatry and a rejection of the God of Israel, which might have been a factor in why he put more importance on his house than God's house.

And it wasn't a stretch for God, who considered a thousand years as one day. But if it were you or me...14 years is a long time to wait for a house to be built! However, outcomes can be positive. For example, the famous king was happy with the wait. He had two new houses, one for God and one for himself!

Narrative: We usually think of a holding pattern or a waiting zone as being something negative; the good effects of the wait are rarely immediate. But once in a while, an outcome is both positive and pleasurable. For example, you had to live with your parents until your dream home was built. Then, you worked to get your Master's degree for two years, resulting in a promotion.

Principle: *Holding patterns* don't always bring hardship and pain; they can also involve looking forward to things that bring pleasure and happiness.
Perspective: Psalm 16:6 "He sees that I am given pleasant brooks and meadows as my share! What a wonderful inheritance!"
Participation: Name the one thing you waited for that brought you the greatest joy. How long did you wait for it?

Elijah held out for 3 ½ years for the rain to end a famine. (I Kings 18)
Background: This prophet was in the Old Testament. He was the sequel to John the Baptist, a hairy, scary, fiery, foreboding messenger of God in the New Testament. Both were social outcasts; neither was in the running for Middle East man of the year!

Scenario: Ahab ruled Israel; Ahab was ruled by his wife, Jezebel, whose name is not usually used in a complementary way. Both had turned away from the true God and turned their country against His laws and practices. They gave allegiance to false deities, the chief of which was Baal and his wife,

Ashtoreth, who were child murderers. Because of this spiritual infidelity, God brought famine to the land, perhaps a symbol of the spiritual dryness of Israel.

Here is Elijah's holding pattern. Due to intensive draught, the famine was forecasted to last three-plus years. In the third year, the prophet was led by God to confront Ahab. (The prophet would probably have rather eaten nails!) But Ahab probably didn't do cartwheels either when the burly bearer of bad tidings showed up. During this time, God provided for Elijah and 100 other prophets by supplying water and raven meat. (The original low carb diet.)

But before the rain came, there was a showdown between the true prophet of God and the 400 false prophets of Baal on Mount Carmel. The contestants gathered at the altar and offered sacrifices to their respective gods. Elijah challenged them to call down fire from heaven to consume the sacrifice, which should have been a piece of cake for Baal, whose name meant Sky God. (Fire, rain, easy assignment!) So his puny prophets called to their God, and nothing happened from morning until noon as they danced around the altar. No answer. Elijah teased them to shout louder. Baal may be deep in thought or traveling, sleeping, or engaged in a business, a euphemism for using the restroom. (No kidding!)

They got the message and were somewhat embarrassed, so they began to cut themselves, bleeding all over the altar. (Maybe they thought they were the sacrifice!) This keeps going until the evening sacrifice. Still, no answer from the powerless pagan god, who couldn't see, hear or speak anyway!

Now it's Elijah's turn. He calls upon his God to send down fire to consume the altar, something God had already done (Judges 6:20-21) and would do. (II Chronicles 7:1-7) He prepares the altar for the evening sacrifice, which had been eliminated by King Jeroboam fifty years before. After placing the bull on it, he commanded that four large jars of water be poured over it, which he repeated twice to ensure it wasn't flammable. And he didn't use kerosene, as some scholars allege. He knew his God would ignite it wet or dry, which He did. The 'True God' had shown the true colors of the pagan god. (Final Score. God - 1 Baal – 0.) The false prophets were all put to death because of the slaughtering of infants in sacrifice to their god and goddess.

It was a 14-mile run to tell Jezebel that his God had overcome her beloved Baal. It was not a stretch; runners could cover 100 miles in two days but usually not have to deal with a queen threatening to kill them! This holding pattern was three and one-half years until the end of the famine became a reality.

Narrative: When God allows for waiting periods in our lives, He is often trying to get our attention; to hear and trust Him to intervene in our situation. Ironically, we often hear God more clearly in a crisis than in a season of comfort!

Principle: *Holding patterns* can make us desperate to hear God and plead with Him to demonstrate His power, often against great odds!

Perspective: II Chronicles 20:17 "But you will not need to fight. Take your places; stand quietly and see the incredible rescue operation God will perform for you, O people of Judah and Jerusalem! Don't be afraid or discouraged! Go out there tomorrow, for the Lord is with you!"

Participation: Describe one or more of your desperate situations when you were the most dependent on God. Did He come through? How?

Elijah waited 40 days for his life to be taken. (I Kings19)
Background: Elijah was riding high on his showdown with the prophets of Baal until Queen Jezebel threatened to take his life within 24 hours. His emotional climate suddenly changed, and he went into a full-blown depression. Yes, people in the Bible, some of the biggest names in God's business, suffered from depression. (In the days before Prozac!)

Elijah had all the classic symptoms; running from reality, loss of appetite, needing to sleep, loss of routine, and contemplating suicide. Is this the same guy who just humiliated 450 now out-of-work prophets? He was instructed to take a 40-day walk to Horeb, the Mountain of God. God met him there, restored his confidence, and told him he was not alone; there were 7000 other God-followers back home who had not bowed down to or kissed Baal. (Yuk!)

God also helped him establish his prophetic routine and choose his successor, who he probably didn't tell about his depression and potential suicide. So what do we learn about *holding patterns* from Elijah, the forerunner to John the Baptist, the camel-hair-clothed, locust-eating prophet of the New Testament?

Narrative: One challenging thing about being human is the letdown we often feel after something significant happens in our life. We can experience letdowns after having a baby and facing post-partum, graduating High School and becoming a Freshman again in college, and returning from a dream vacation to a job that is a nightmare. Pastors know the feeling after an exhilarating Sunday and coming into the office on Monday to start the process all over again.

Principle: *Holding patterns* can come after a great moment of success and be followed by an acute sense of failure.

Perspective: I Kings 19:10-12 "He replied, I have worked very hard for the Lord God of the heavens, but the people of Israel have broken their covenant with you and torn down your altars and killed your prophets, and only I am left; and now they are trying to kill me too." "Go out and stand before me on the mountain, the Lord told him. And as Elijah stood there, the Lord passed by and a mighty windstorm hit the mountain; it was such a terrible blast that the rocks were torn loose, but the Lord was not in the wind. After the wind, there was an earthquake, but the Lord was not in the earthquake. And after the earthquake, there was a fire, but the Lord was not in the fire. And after the fire, there was the sound of a gentle whisper."

Participation: Have you ever experienced a letdown and defeat after a great success? What were the signs of your being let down and defeated? Did God rescue you?

Namaan waited for obedience to result in a miracle. (II Kings 5:1-14)

Background: Elisha is now the prophet of choice, touring the country with the help of hebrewhotels.com, doing the same incredible miracles his predecessor Elijah did. (After all, he had twice the power by request.) His reputation spread like a grass fire in Midland, Texas, even to the courts of Syria. Namaan, the king of Syria, heard about him from his wife's servant girl, an Israeli prisoner of war. The king was also a leper. The first holding pattern is based on how long he would be a leper. Usually, it was forever. The second one was how long it would be before he could be healed. Usually for a leper, it was never.

So the king writes a letter sent by camel express, no less, to the prophet, who he is sure is in on a plot to exterminate him. And Namaan pulls up in front of Elisha's abode with a gleaming chariot and Budweiser stallions ready for the nice, neat little miracle. Abba Cadabra! And the leprosy was gone! But that was not the way the show was scripted.

Instead, the mighty king is told to bathe in a dirty river. But, unfortunately, the River Jordan is a river with brown water for all its positive publicity.

His royal majesty was a leper but still the king, so he was duly insulted. He rattles off two Syrian rivers that are much cleaner and wonders why he can't take his bath in those. "Aw, c'mon, Naaman," his comrades scolded him. "Want to be clean or not?" Thus incentivizing him to do as he was told, dip himself in the muddy waters, not once but seven times! Guess what? No leprosy! The once belligerent king is muddy but elated and claims that the God of Israel is the only true God in the entire world.

Narrative: From childhood, we get orders to obey when we would rather not and often don't! And even though it may be good for us, we rebel, not realizing that obedience brings about a positive outcome. (Like having to practice the piano for an hour every single day!)

Principle: *Holding patterns* can teach us new things about God and obedience even when it involves things we would rather not do.

Perspective: I Samuel 15:22 "Samuel replied, Has the Lord as much pleasure in your burnt offerings and sacrifices as in your obedience?"

Participation: Think of an instance where God asked you to do something unpleasant you didn't want to do, but you did it anyway. What was the outcome?

Hezekiah knew he would die in 15 years. (II Kings:1-11)

Background: Hezekiah, who incidentally wasn't one of the Minor Prophets, was a good and godly king. But, he became ill, and the prophet Isaiah, the minister of visitation, called on him with a death sentence. (Cheer up, you're on your way out!) But Hezekiah asked God to honor his godly reign by extending his life. I'm not sure you can use the barter system with God, but it was worth a shot, right? It worked. God promises Hezekiah 15 more years of life by using boiled figs, no less, which would either kill or cure you! This homemade remedy lengthened his life from 37 to 52 years.

Interestingly enough, Hezekiah fathered a child during those added years whose name was Manasseh, which sounds a little like a mess that the kid made of the kingdom. Hezekiah also gave a group of Babylonian dignitaries a 'White House Tour' showing them all the kingdom's treasures they would pillage after his death. When questioned about it, he simply dismissed the threat knowing that it wouldn't happen in his lifetime, forget the impact on others!

This is one of the more intriguing *holding patterns* in scripture. Why? Because the person in the midst of it was able to count down the exact number of days before he died, something most of us are not privy to. Knowing when the holding pattern would end undoubtedly shaped his life and affected his choices, like showing the enemy his treasure and fathering a child who led his nation into betraying their God.

Narrative: When someone knows they have limited time to live, their whole life is turned upside down. The days are fleeting, and every minute is precious. You are shaken when you find out that your friend has terminal cancer. All the aspects of daily life become more important. We embrace those closest to us in new ways. Life passes before our eyes; we face our own mortality and assess what is essential and how we live our life. And we are more determined to give life our best shot regardless of how much time we've got!

Principle: *Holding patterns* can cause us to re-assess life goals because we don't know how much time we have left!
Perspective: Matthew 17:22-23 "One day while they were still in Galilee, Jesus told them, I am going to be betrayed into the power of those who will kill me, and on the third day afterwards, I will be brought back to life again. And the disciple's hearts were filled with sorrow and dread."
Participation: Have you ever known someone who knew precisely long they had to live? How did it affect how they lived out the rest of their life? How did that affect you?

Manasseh wasted a 67-year lifetime. (II Kings 21:1-18)
Background: The spoiled brat who became the successor to the throne for fifty-five years was one of the longest-reigning and most wicked rulers in all Israeli history.

Under the influence of a pagan mother, often the case with the sons of Solomon, Manasseh undid all the good his father had done. And the Babylonians returned to Jerusalem not to tour the Temple but to burn it down and horrify the people. They were ultimately taken captive and freighted off to Babylon, where the horrid king finally submitted to the God he had forsaken and tried to undo some of the damage. But unfortunately, it would take his grandson, Josiah, to continue the too-little-too-late reform movement.

Manasseh was 12 years old when he came to reign and died at 67, young by modern standards. His life was no doubt shortened by his own apostasy and wicked rule. (But what would you really expect putting a pre-adolescent in charge of the country?) His holding pattern was one of waiting for the other shoe to drop. God's judgment was about to come upon His people for their blatant disobedience to Him and His laws which his indulgent but godly father had taught him. Godlier kings had lived for a shorter time. But in this case, God allows a king and people more time to turn to Him and live better lives.

Narrative: Sometimes, life is shortened by making poor choices in diet, exercise, and general life patterns. On the other hand, our Maker may extend our life because He wants us to learn things that promote our welfare and a better life.

Principle: *Holding patterns* can be lengthened by our failure to make the needed life corrections.
Perspective: II Peter 3:9 "He isn't really being slow about His promised return, even though it sometimes seems that way, But He is waiting for the good reason that He is not willing that any should perish, and He is giving more time for sinners to repent."
Participation: When has God been especially patient with you as His child? What lessons did you learn?

Nehemiah waited for 52 days for a project to be completed.
(Nehemiah 1:2-4)
Background: He was likely a young man when he was taken captive in Babylon and promoted to cupbearer for Persia's King, Artaxerxes. Now make no mistake; this was not a run-of-the-mill position; the cupbearer didn't offer you an array of porcelain teacups. Instead, Nehemiah sipped the wine out of an old goblet before the king did to ensure that his enemies hadn't poisoned it! If the cupbearer didn't fall over dead after a sip and a swallow, the king was free to enjoy the wine!

The eyewitness historical narrative records Nehemiah was compelled by God to do something about the dastardly conditions in his homeland of Judah. His people were afflicted, the city walls were broken down, and the gates were burned with fire. Jerusalem had become a junkyard.

According to chapter two, we know that in the same year he came to the palace, the king notices his wine-tasting sipper isn't his bright, cheerful, extroverted self and asks him about it. Nehemiah answered, "Wouldn't you be sad, too, if your hometown was in shambles?" And lo and behold, the King asks him how he can help; no doubt a result of prayer and fasting.

Then the trembling cupbearer gives the king a list of materials from the pre-Lowes lumber yard, and guess what? He gets what he needs plus time off and a letter of reference commanding all the right people to cooperate with the restoration effort. So he makes the 551-mile trip to Persepolis, the capital city. Weather permitting, try that on foot or by donkey deluxe, at about three miles a day. That computes to one-hundred and eighty-four days in Middle East heat!

If it's not taxing enough to travel that distance with the threat of being hi-jacked and finding your home in complete disarray, you have enemies living next door. There were three *holding patterns* for this future Governor of Israel. Waiting to ask the king for help, completing the long journey home, and rebuilding the walls in only 52 days, all while facing the opposition of the enemies of the Jews trying to re-establish and occupy their city. Imagine that!

Times haven't changed much since 444 BC. This historic rescue effort took place 2500 years ago. Each holding pattern was filled with apprehension and angst. Would the king not understand? Could the captives make the long trip home in the heat? Would the nasty neighbors get a court order to stop the re-construction project? By the way, Nehemiah was rewarded with two governorships due to being on hold. It pays to wait!

Narrative: Everyone on earth faces a deadline. From learning to walk to potty training, graduating to landing a good job, completing homework, and turning in a time card, people live by meeting deadlines. But one good thing, the sooner you meet the deadline, the sooner your holding pattern is over!

Principle: *Holding patterns* often center on meeting deadlines, usually under pressure!
Perspective: II Timothy 4:7 "I have fought long and hard for my Lord, and through it all, I have kept true to Him. And now the time has come for me to stop fighting and rest."
Participation: Identify a major deadline you had to meet, what happened, and remember how you handled the pressure.

Esther waited for six months for her people to be saved from destruction. (Esther 7-8)
Background: This book was written about an Old Testament Cinderella, whose name meant Star. The 167 verses are loaded with drama, suspense, war, and conquest! (Moviestar, Angelina Jolie, would have won the Oscar for it!)

Esther (Hadassah) was a Jewess imported to Babylon, which became Persia in BC 539. Her parents had both died, and her Uncle Mordecai subsequently adopted her. (One can only imagine his nickname!) Long story short, the current queen, Vashti, resigned under protests for refusing to show off her body to a bunch of drunken providence presidents. Actually, she was fired. Thus, the Miss Persia Beauty Pageant was invented to find a replacement queen. (Uncle Mordecai enters his niece, Esther, and she wins!)

She was immediately thrust into a holding pattern; she had to go thru a whole year regimen of treatments. Six months of face and body creams, six months of perfumes, things for beautifying women. (We do know it takes women a while to get ready!) Well, no headline news; Esther won, hands down. So this complete unknown becomes queen of a nation stretched from India to Ethiopia, comprised of 127 provinces.

One of the things unknown about her was that she wasn't a hometown girl or a graduate of Persia State with a degree in cosmetology; she was a *Jewess no less.* But the title didn't make her co-ruler of the kingdom. Instead, she was more like a trophy wife. She could only see the king in the royal courtroom when he extended his scepter. To do otherwise would mean her death. (It makes you wonder how many candle-light dinners they had together, doesn't it?)

Thus, she waited for the right time to approach her royal husband, who said yes with his wand. She proceeded to tell him about one of his high-ranking officials plotting to kill her people and divulging her ethnic identity for the first time. Her book deals with the annihilation of the Jewish people by foreign powers.

This resulted from a long feud between the descendants of Esau, the Amalekites, and the Israelites. Haman, the predator of her people, was exposed, so he didn't hang around for long! Esther and her people had the excruciatingly long wait for Haman's edict to be reversed in favor of saving, not killing, the Israelites. This resulted in a victory over her enemies. Purim, a Christmas/Thanksgiving-like celebration commemorated God's mighty intervention due to a Persian Queen who trusted God, the King of the universe.

Narrative: Often, we see life in retrospect. As they say, hindsight is 20-20! So we usually don't know what we accomplished in a holding pattern until it's over. Then it makes sense. "Oh, now I see" we say. And fulfilling God's bigger purpose isn't reserved only for beauty queens; all the King's kids are included in the plan. Remember, God is working out a bigger plan and has a bigger picture we can't usually see until later on.

Principle: *Holding patterns* are necessary to prepare us for special assignments which have us in the right place at the right time to fulfill God's bigger purposes.
Perspective: Ephesians 3:20 "Now glory be to God, who by His mighty power at work within us is able to do far more than we would ever dare to ask or even dream of, infinitely beyond our highest prayers, desires, thoughts or hopes."
Participation: Have you ever been in a situation that didn't make sense at the time but allowed you to see God's broader purpose and bigger plan later on? What was that greater work? Did this possibly happen more than once? Explain.

Job waited 40 years between losing his first family and starting a second one. (Job 42)
Background: Job purportedly lived at the beginning of civilization. He was an entrepreneurial agriculturist, one of the wealthiest men of his time. He, like Noah, was one of the few righteous men in a pagan culture. So, he had God's attention and Satan's attention. The Evil One challenged God to remove all the blessing of material things, family, and health, predicting that Job would turn on and betray his God. Although it was a test from God, his three so-called friends blamed it on him.

Biblical scholars place this discourse on human suffering at the beginning of civilization. Why? Suffering became a permanent part of life due to our first parent's fall into sin. Thus, Job has become the prototype for personal losses in the physical, economic, familial, and spiritual realms.

He loses his children, all seven at once in a freak accident, all of his livestock and camel keepers in one fell swoop, and gets the worst case of Old Testament shingles possible, head to toe in boils; and to boot, his wife tells him to "curse God and die." (I mean, would we really blame her?)

But though he didn't take her advice, he probably felt God had turned His back on him. In fact, he spent 40 chapters trying to figure out what hit him and why it happened. The question was arrogantly answered by three former best friends who explained it this way: Hey dude, you messed up; God doesn't afflict sinless people! But, of course, the Holy Book says there are no sinless people and doesn't promise that righteous people won't suffer. Job was righteous, and he did suffer. Seventeen conditions afflicted him, including severe itching, dramatic weight loss, hallucinations, infected skin, and a raging fever.

Narrative: Understandably, Job was drowning in a sea of suffering and subsequent sorrows. We don't know the exact duration of the divine testing. But what we do know is God had Satan on a leash, restricting his power. The one thing God wanted Job to know was that He was in charge of everything in his life. The only honest answer to why Job got a bad deal was to see if this godly man would still trust God if he lost everything. His book is called a theodicy; to defend God amidst calamity. Job learned it's not *what* you know; it's *who* you know; in this case, it was God, the creator, and sustainer of all life. Any holding pattern involving this kind of pain in all aspects of life would seem endless.

However, one of the potentially misleading elements of this book is that an unfortunate story always has a very happy ending. Not everyone who suffers has one. This one did because Job got back everything, lived another a hundred and forty years to enjoy it, and became a great grandfather. (I'll bet his wife was glad he didn't take her advice, huh?)

But, even though Mr. and Mrs. Job got a wonderful re-set, they didn't get to start where they left off with grown children; they had to conceive and give birth to them. It must have been a little like when some parents sent their oldest to college and re-decorated the nursery the same year. We can only wonder how the new parents felt, starting over on a task they had already completed once! So, even though Job's story had a happy ending, his new life had a slow beginning.

Principle: *Holding patterns* are often ones we can't explain by human insight but cause us to know and place more trust in the one who allows them to happen.
Perspective: Job 1:10-11 "You have always protected him and his home and his property from all harm. You have prospered everything he does. Look how rich he is! No wonder he worships you! But just take away his wealth, and you'll see him curse you to your face."
Participation: Ever had something happen in your life that you could never explain apart from supernatural intervention? Begin to keep a record of these God sightings.

The Nation of Israel

Some of God's people waited 40 years to enter Canaan. (Numbers 13:17-18,32)

Background: Ready, set, go into the Promised Land, the reason for leaving Egypt. This was not the sentiment of God's frozen-chosen people. Ah, sure, we trust God completely to bring us into the land of milk and honey but just in case, let's check it out before we go there. Calling all spies! They called twelve, one for every tribe of Israel, for a spy mission led by Joshua and Caleb.

Verdict: *Let's not go,* got ten votes. *Let's go,* only two votes. God is disgusted with His people, to say the least. He tells them that because they have seen His glory and miracles in Egypt and in the wilderness and they tempted Him, none of them would enter the land except Joshua, Caleb, and their children. All the rest of them would die in the wilderness. At least Moses wouldn't be the only one to die before going in. Sadly, it wouldn't be the last time they would be intimidated by giants they believed God could not over-power. (Goliath, by the way, had a whole bunch of descendants).

Their holding pattern was 40 years in duration. Imagine knowing exactly how long your holding pattern would be! Those days would be filled with disappointment knowing that your innocent children would have a life in Canaan without you. But here's the kicker; God made these days as livable as possible for his disbelieving, disobedient people. The scriptural account records that He fed them with angel food, gave them clean water, and protected their sandals from wearing out.

Narrative: We've all been in a stop-over in the journey of life where we wonder how on earth we will make it until the next payday or have enough food to feed our family. Perhaps the nation of Israel had the same question when they messed up and were relegated to a wilderness for forty years. So what were they going to do now? You guessed it; God cared for the physical needs of hunger, thirst, and footwear. God is not only big and strong enough to care for us when we do the right things but also when we don't! Sometimes, our wilderness isn't a result of our disobedience; it just comes anyway. (Job didn't mess up, and look what he got!) Either way, remember, God's care is always there, everywhere.

Principle: During our *holding patterns*, God doesn't stop caring for us and supplying our needs.
Perspective: Psalm 78:37-38 "Their hearts were far away. They did not keep their promises. Yet, He was merciful, forgave their sins, and didn't destroy them all. Many and many a time, He held back His anger."
Participation: Ever feel that God has deserted you and stopped caring for you in a holding pattern? In time, did you see that He did come through?

God's people waited 20 years for their altar of worship to be returned. (I Samuel 4-6)
Background: The Ark of the Covenant or the Ark of Testimony had its origins in the book of Exodus shortly after the Ten Commandments were given. It was really fancy, and what's more, it was portable and able to be carried from place to place; worship for people on the go. It contained Aaron's rod, a jar of manna, the Ten Commandments, and the first five books of the Torah scroll. It was carried out in advance of the people of Israel and their army.

So, it was a gigantic deal when it was stolen! The Philistines, those proverbial pests, had the audacity not only to take it but put it in the temple of their pagan god, Dagon. Funny thing; when they got up in the morning, their not-so-great god was face down on the ground. (Think there might have been a clue?)

The other humorous part of the story is that God afflicted Israel's enemies with emerods. They are better known to us as hemorrhoids. (I guess God got to the seat of their problem!)

God allowed the Ark to be taken because God's people were unwilling to give up their allegiance to false gods and trust the power of the true God. It finally came home, and God's power was returned to the Israelites, who finally defeated the Ark thieves themselves.

Narrative: Often, we get flack from difficult people who dislike what we believe and become antagonistic to us personally. So we ask God, why me, why now, why them? God answers the question with one of His own, why not?

Principle: *Holding patterns* can be easier for us knowing that God will deal with the people who make life difficult.
Perspective: Matthew 5:43-44 "There is a saying, 'Love your friends and hate your enemies.' But I say: Love those who persecute you!"
Participation: Has God helped you deal with people who made your life harder? If yes, how? Do you make life harder for others and need to change your response?

God's people waited 73 years for their captivity to end.
(II Kings 17-18; II Chronicles 29-36)
Background: Israel was finally taken captive by Assyria in 721 BC. The Northern Kingdom lasted about 200 years. Every one of its kings walked in the way of wicked Jeroboam, who introduced golden calf worship to keep the people of the North from going to Jerusalem. And it wasn't like God didn't warn

them. They had a whole host of prophets hit them square between the eyes with the truth. They warned them that God would close down the country if they didn't get their act together. (Possibly during an Old Testament pandemic?) It was a little like the billboard that quotes God, "Don't make me come down there!" The last king of Israel even tried to buy the Assyrians off and made a clandestine deal with Egypt to stave off a pending judgment. But it was too little, too late. Moreover, the enemy infiltrated the people of Israel with pagans to weaken its spiritual and moral resolve.

Israel had two major *holding patterns*; three years under siege by the King of Assyria and 70 years when 2,790 people were deported to Assyria. Assyrians were known to skin their prisoners alive, cut off their hands and feet, pull out their tongues, and make a mound of human skulls to inspire terror. (It doesn't sound like living next door to the Brady Bunch, does it?) But God got Israel's attention, and they returned home in more ways than one. They learned to depend on God and look beyond their problem to see the His provision.

Narrative: God still uses the same methods He has always used with the people He loves. There is an old saying, "If God seems far away, guess who moved?" When we go our own way, He loves us too much to let us stay that way. He will do whatever it takes to get us back on track. We might think He is too hard on us, but we must remember that our relationship with Him causes Him to do what is best for us. God will do whatever it takes to bring us back to Himself and cause us to depend on His resources more than our own.

Principle: When *holding patterns* are hard, we can choose to focus more on the provision than the problem, possibly making them easier.

Perspective: II Kings 6:16 “Don’t be afraid!” Elisha told him. “For our army is bigger than theirs!”
Participation: Can you name a time in your life when you witnessed God’s provision as more significant than the problem?

God’s people waited through two years of famine before being conquered by the Babylonians. (II Kings 24:1-25, II Chronicles 36)
Background: Judah, Israel's little sister, the Southern Kingdom, failed to learn from her older sister. Instead, she plunged headlong into idolatry, calf worship, sex cults, and offering her children as living sacrifices to Molech. Judah had plenty of time to turn around on the road marked dead-end, but she kept going headlong into the swamp. Jeremiah predicted it would last seventy years. Seventy years was one for every year they failed to keep the Sabbath (II Chronicles 36:21)

So Babylonia was used as a tool of judgment against God's delinquent daughter. Babylonian captivity came in three sections. (605 BC, 597 BC, 586 BC.) But even in punishment, God was merciful and patient with His errant children.

Narrative: Think for a minute. What would it be like to know how long your holding pattern would be? Several factors are worth noting. Maybe God doesn't always tell us how long our holding pattern will be. Why? Because we might procrastinate and put off doing what we want to do until the last minute. (Like Christmas shopping or studying for finals). The other reason might be we’d become discouraged and give up.

When we are in the middle of a holding pattern, we are more likely to take a good look at our lives and evaluate how we can improve them. But we don’t like change and often put off self-assessment. We are also prone to avoid altering our lifestyle and choices because staying the same is easier and less work. After all, our distorted logic tells us that we've gotten along pretty well so far; we'll make it okay. So we wonder: Is it more painful to change or to stay the same? *Holding patterns* may make it less painful to change and more productive in the long run! It's up to us to choose.

Principle: Our *holding patterns* can often motivate us to make changes in our lives for our good.
Perspective: Psalm 126:5-6 "Those who sow tears shall reap joy. Yes, they go out weeping, carrying seed for sowing and return singing, carrying their sheaves."
Participation: As you reflect on your life, was there a time of waiting that forced you to make changes that otherwise might not have happened?

Poetical Books
Psalms
Background of David and the Psalms
David is best known for being a man after God's own heart, which is pretty good billing for an adulterer and a murderer! Nevertheless, David, the seventh son in the family of Jessie, the great-grandson of Ruth, rose from warding off wolves to bringing down giants; from tending a flock to ruling a country. David was one of the greatest kings who ever lived, but his 40 years of office were marked by discord and unrest due to his own out-of-control lust. Yet his reign became a prototype of Christ, who would rule forever on the throne of his father, David.

Most of the Psalms written by this man were characterized by his problems and the provision by his God who could solve them. Moreover, Psalms were scripture set to music, natural for a man who was an exceptional musician. (Probably first chair harpist in the Jerusalem symphony.)

Of all the writers of scriptures, David gives the most permission to let it all out with God; anger, resentment, despair, failure, disgust with enemies, insecurity, confusion, and fatigue in waiting.

So we can relate to and learn from the shepherd-king who messed up, fessed up, and taught us how to be honest with our God in the face of life's realities and how He can help us live through and get through life's *holding patterns*.

Theme: The prevalence of wickedness (Psalm 13:1) (KJV) David

"How long will you forget me? How long will you hide your face from me?" Saul was most likely hunting David. His cry for help began with prayer and ended with praise to God, whom he realizes has not deserted him. David focused on fact over feeling. His God was greater than the cowardly king.

Theme: The crucifixion of Christ (Psalm 22:1) (KJV) David

"Why hast thou forsaken me; Why art thou so far from helping me"? The controversial Psalm was based on differing views on whether this is a prophetic picture of the suffering and death of Christ or not. Within the Old Testament context, however, the description equivocates precisely with the actual historical accounts of the events in the life of Christ as cited in the New Testament accounts. (Matthew 27:36, Mark 15:34, John 19:24, Hebrews 2:12)

Theme: Devotion in God's house of worship (Psalm 27:13) (KJV) David
"I had fainted unless I had believed to see the goodness of the Lord in the land of the living." The first part of the Psalm is joyous and triumphant; the second part is sad and plaintive. The writer has regained hope, having just been saved from sinking into despair by the employment of faith. The sentiment is one of a martyr at the end of his life. Quite possibly, it was during the rebellion of David's son, Absalom, that the writer complains of rejection by those closest to him.

Theme: Dedication of the Lord's temple (Psalm 30:5) (KJV) David
"For His anger endureth but a moment; weeping may endure for a night, but joy cometh in the morning." It is a song commemorating deliverance from a great danger. Grief is turned into gladness ending in a burst of joy. It was composed at the height of Hebrew poetry and used for recitation in the temple centered on the altar's dedication after David had sinned by numbering the people. It was sung as part of what would be considered an Old Testament Thanksgiving service. It is still recited at the Feast of Dedication in the fall of the year.

Theme: A song of trust (Psalm 31:10) (KJV) David
"For life is spent with anguish and my years with sighing; my strength faileth because of iniquity and my bones consumed." The Psalm is one in which the writer cries out for help in the presence of danger and trouble. It ends with a eulogy of God's goodness and exhortation for God-fearers. It has been linked to David's persecution under Saul or Absolom's rebellion.

Theme: Trust in God (Psalm 37:7) (KJV) David
"Rest in the Lord, wait patiently for Him; do not fret because of the one who prospers in his way, who brings wicked devices to pass." This is an alphabetical Psalm where each section begins with a letter of the Hebrew alphabet. It is considered a type of poem that can easily be remembered and reassure minds disturbed by the earthly prosperity of the wicked. The theme of the Psalm is retribution for the wicked and reward for the righteous.

Theme: Praise to God for a great deliverance (Psalm 40:1) (KJV) David
"I waited patiently for the Lord, and He inclined unto me and heard my cry." The writer begins with specific praise for deliverance and then moves to general praise for His wondrous works throughout the history of His people. David's response is not in the formality of religious tradition but a complete devotion to God as evidence of his intimate relationship with Him. Thus, the psalmist complains about his enemies but affirms God as his Helper and Defender who won't be late coming to his rescue.

Theme: A poem of fervent devotion (Psalm 62:5) (KJV) David
"My soul, wait for thou only upon God, for my expectation is from Him." The Psalmist cries for help from a man in a high position whose enemies try to destroy His people. He expresses his ultimate assurance that his adversaries cannot succeed. He writes to inspire confidence in the people when the revolt of his son, Absolom, was imminent. He uses the term Selah, a sequel to a comma in the narrative, translated as Amen.

Theme: A Psalm of suffering (Psalm 69:3) (KJV) David
"I am weary of crying, mine eyes fail while I wait for God." A man deals with his own sin. Jeremiah could have written it. It is often connected with Psalm 55. Paul referenced it in Romans 11:9. David most likely wrote it when Adonijah, Solomon's step-brother, tried to go through Bathsheba to arrange for him to become the king instead of Solomon.

Theme: A historical Psalm (Psalm 77:8) (KJV) Asaph
"Has His unfailing love vanished forever?" The writer speaks for his country, complaining of their departure from the Lord, but his confidence in God's unfailing mercy is based on his outstanding track record. Selah once again infers amen, an agreement with what the Psalmist wrote.

Theme: Israel's waywardness (Psalm 82:2) (KJV) Asaph
"How long will you judge unjustly and accept the person of the wicked." The context is that of God standing amidst the angelic host of heaven denouncing the unjust judges who control His people on earth. The writer prods God to take immediate action.

Theme: A lifelong sufferer (Psalm 88:14-15) (KJV) Heman, the Ezrahite
"Lord, why castest off my soul, why hidest thy face from me. I am afflicted and ready to die from my youth up: while I suffer the terrors, I am distracted." This is the most mournful of all the Psalms. Job is thought to be the potential author of this Psalm because of the tone of complaint. All the complaints are personal and indicate longsuffering. The writer seems to be without hope but does not fall away from God upon whom he calls and to whom he prays.

Theme: God's oath (Psalm 88:14) (KJV) Heman, the Ezrahite
"How long, Lord, will you hide yourself forever, shall thy wrath burn like fire?" The first portion of the Psalm centers on singing praise to God, culminating in the Davidic Covenant. But the covenant appears to have been annulled; everything that is happening runs contrary to God's promises. The question of the writer is, how long is this to continue? The Psalmist holds God to His promise to deliver Israel and the Davidic House from their calamities and to do it promptly! He is to prove himself, especially in the eyes of his enemies.

Theme: An ordinary Psalm (Psalm 90:10) (KJV) Moses
"Seventy years are given us! And some may even live to eighty. But even the best of these years are often empty and filled with pain; soon they disappear, and we are gone." The writing is an ancient one attributed to someone as old as Moses. It begins with meditation, moves to the complaint, and begins a prayer in verse 12. Here Moses is described as a man of God in Deuteronomy 33:1, Joshua 14:6, and Ezra 3:2. It reads like a travelogue of one's journey with God through a long life**,** 120 years for Moses, far beyond the 70 or 80 years the life spans referenced in this Psalm.

Significantly, the writer of the first five books of the Bible began with God's everlastingness having brought the world into being. Moses's life can be traced through the narrative; all the events, the emotions, the triumphs, and tragedies all through which his God has brought him to the brink of the Promised Land, which he was not allowed to enter. Moses knew that his God would never forsake the works of His hands. He didn't die a natural death; God just took him to heaven.

Theme: A nature Psalm (Psalm 104:27-28) (KJV) Anonymous "Every one of these depends on you to give them daily food. You supply it, and they gather it. You open wide your hand to feed them and they are satisfied with all your bountiful provision." The writer scribes one of the most beautiful Psalms describing God's creation and care of all that dwell within it, people and animals. It serves as a reminder that God does everything in His time and on His terms.

Theme: Thanksgiving for return from captivity
(Psalm 126:6) (KJV) Anonymous
"He that goeth forth and weepeth, bearing precious seed shall doubtless come again rejoicing bring his sheaves with him." The Psalm was written after Judah's return from 70 years in captivity. The complaining stops as God's people recall the great things God has done for them. Theirs is a spirit of hilarity. The sub-theme could be: As you have done it before, Lord, do it again! The people consider their reaping and weeping to result in a harvest of joy!

Theme: A penitential Psalm a cry for mercy (Psalm 139:5-6) (KJV) David "I wait for the Lord, my soul doth wait, and in His word do I hope; my soul waited for the Lord more than they that watch for the morning." The cry of Israel is in extreme distress. The word penitential is the basis of a penitentiary, a place of confinement for breaking the law. This is precisely Israel's condition; she is in captivity for disobeying God and His law. Here she acknowledges her sins and prays for mercy and forgiveness, which culminates in a confident expectation from God, something they watch for like a watchman waits for the morning, which they know ultimately comes after the night.

Summary of the Psalms

The *holding patterns* of the Psalms appear to be distinct from most of the others we have seen in the Old Testament up to this point. They center around the terms, cry out and wait.

Nearly all of them have to do with a personal rather than a physical crisis. For example, David deals with a jealous, somewhat deranged King Saul. Israel is putting up with enemies trying to take her land and enslave her, believing that God has forsaken her in her personal struggles as a nation.

Honesty and realness describe the psalmists who make no pretense of their anger, confusion, impatience, or desire for vengeance. But, they also include expressions of thanks, praise, and joy. Moreover, this gives the rest of us permission to feel and express our emotions in the same ways. Our God understands and responds calmly and nonreactively; He can take it.

Narrative: Everyone needs someone they can vent to, let it all out, and blow off steam. Real friends let you do that. But they are often few and far between. If only we could realize that the Holy Trinity is made up of potentially three of our closest friends. They know all about us, understand us, and still love us anyway. But, we often avoid getting close to them; we are intimidated by their power and position. So we have a lot of company when it comes to needing to be ourselves and be honest. Men and women throughout biblical life faced this same dilemma and found God to be just the one they could talk to about the really frustrating and troubling issues within the circumstances of life.

Principle: In the *holding patterns* of life, we have permission to let God know exactly how we feel about waiting; something He already knows and understands anyway.

Perspective: Psalm 69:3 "I have wept until I am exhausted, my throat is dry and hoarse; my eyes are swollen with weeping, waiting for my God to act."
Participation: Ever felt fearful of telling God exactly how you feel? Why did you hold back these feelings from Him? Have you acquired more honesty with Him as you have progressed in your spiritual life?

Proverbs
Waiting in the process of parenting (Proverbs) 22:6 (KJV) "Train up a child in the way they should go and when they are old, they will not depart from it." This is one of the most puzzling proverbs for parents. Why? First, we don't know which way to train a child to go; each child is different. Also, if they reject their faith, we don't know if and when they will return to it.

The thought in the Hebrew mind was that of customizing the instruction of a child according to their temperament, personality, and learning style. In other words, when it comes to Christian education, one size does not fit all. It seems unfair, doesn't it? You have your first child, get it all figured out, then God sends you the second one who is entirely different, and you have to start all over! How many people have learned real dependency on the Lord after becoming parents? As to the "when they are old," the parent hopes they live long enough to see the child return to what they have taught them.

Narrative: Every age has parents who have anguished over wayward, delinquent kids who departed from the faith they grew up with, got into a heap of trouble, and shattered the dreams they had for them. Parents often feel guilt and failure. There is no guarantee that kids raised in a religious home won't mess up, take detours or reject their faith. But God promises us that whatever truth is imparted into the child's life will always remain and that when they are adults, they will realize it's essential and incorporate it back into their lives.

Principle: *Holding patterns* involve children who may depart from what we have taught them.
Perspective: Psalm 103:17-18 "But the loving-kindness of the Lord is from everlasting to everlasting to those who reverence Him; His salvation is to children's children of those who are faithful to His covenant and remember to obey Him!"
Participation: Did one of your children turn away from their faith? How long did it take the wayward child to return, or did they? Are you still waiting? If so, why not find another parent to talk this out with and pray together about it?

Ecclesiastes
Waiting for satisfaction (Ecclesiastes 2:22-23) (NIV)
"What does a man get for all the toil and anxious striving with which he labors under the sun? His days are work, pain, and grief; even at night, his mind does not rest. This, too, is meaningless." Solomon must have been a type-A personality, the driven CEO of Israel who stayed awake at night reviewing his stock portfolios and putting too many hours in at the palace. But then who wants to discuss how their day went with 700 wives? (No wonder he couldn't sleep!)

At any rate, Solomon finds himself in a holding pattern that extends to his entire working life, 40 years at least. So he asks the question many modern executives ask; is it all worth it? Or is this all there is? (If it isn't and this is all there is, then it is all meaningless.)

Remember, Solomon started out well but didn't finish well. When he cut God out of his life, he began a godless pursuit of wealth, pleasure, wild women, and wine. God does not do well with the competition; he rewards rejection with retribution. So the wise man became a wise guy whose life became futile with no purpose. His self-caused consequences changed his philosophy of life to nihilism; the rejection of all religious and moral values and the loss of all hope.

Narrative: How often have you and I become bored with our faith, trusting ourselves and our resources to get through life? Since Abraham and Sarah replaced God's plan with their own, we've also sought other sources, all the lesser alternatives which prove deficient and defective. Yet, in these times, God is there with us while we wait; He waits for us to return to Him, pass Go and collect all the help and resources we need to win the game of life. Of course, God's plan would have worked better, but our need to control and be in charge makes us learn the hard way.

Principle: Sometimes, we look to someone other than God for help to get through our time of waiting.

Perspective: Joshua 24:14 "So revere Jehovah and serve Him in sincerity and truth. Put away forever the idols your ancestors worshipped when they lived beyond the Euphrates River and in Egypt. Worship the Lord alone."

Participation: In your holding pattern, did you look to other resources to get through it? If so, what things did you turn to? What did this experience teach you?

Waiting for the kids to grow up (Ecclesiastes 12:1)

"Remember your Creator in the days of your youth, before the days of trouble come and the years approach when you will say, I find no pleasure in them." No one knows how long it takes for someone to grow up, right?

This verse adds the caveat that corresponds with Solomon's proverb about the kids departing from what they have been taught but returning to it later in life. Finding no pleasure in them is the same thing as departing. His depiction of getting old explains what happens later when he returns to his faith as a youth. It involves the regrets and despondency this once God-fearing King pondered. He realizes his life is futile because he lost his close relationship with God, the true source of wisdom and a satisfying and fulfilling life.

Narrative: Every child growing into adulthood enters a holding pattern as they cross the bridge of adolescence into adulthood. Psychologists tell us that it is a longer holding pattern for boys than girls; females are more social and mature much faster. (Sorry, guys!) However, most of us know people who have never grown up; they are still stalled on the bridge.

Growing up is not optional, but maturity depends on the choices made in the process. As naïve parents, we thought we would have it made once our kids walked across the high school graduation platform. Little did we realize that the most significant life decisions were ahead when we would have less control over life's situations. The adolescent holding pattern is marked by immaturity, impatience, and indomitable thinking! The astounding reality is that many people remain in this holding pattern much longer than they need to or is necessary. They stop growing up and get stuck on the treadmill of development. They remain adolescents into adulthood, sometimes for life! (Know anyone like that?) The decisions made in these years can literally determine the course of our entire life.

Principle: Sometimes, we get stuck in the developmental process, and the Lord waits until we are ready to move on to the next stage.
Perspective: Hebrews 5:12-13 "You have been Christians a long time now, and you ought to be teaching others, but instead you have dropped back to the place where you need someone to teach you all over again the very first principles in God's Word. You are like babies who can drink only milk, not old enough for solid food."
Participation: Have you ever been in one of those stuck zones? How long did it take you to get out of it? What did you need to learn while you were in it?

Song of Solomon
Waiting to find the right relationship (Song of Solomon 8:4)
"I charge you daughters that you don't stir or wake my love until he pleases."
Background: This controversial book has a single holding pattern appropriately situated in the last chapter. Song of Solomon has been viewed skeptically since its inception because it deals with the topic no one likes to talk about; *sex*. (The truth, of course, is that everyone talks about it!) After all, it is one of those things God saw and said was "very good." So Solomon wasn't ashamed to bring up the subject. (After all, any man with nearly a thousand partners, including the wives and the concubines, would have been an expert on the subject, don't you think?) Solomon was the master of the metaphor, which he used prolifically in all three of his writings.

After seven chapters, he quotes one of his wives describing the male and female anatomy, the lure of love, and the satisfaction of the most intimate relationship between two human beings.

The woman speaking could well be his first wife, believed to be the daughter of Pharoah, a young adolescent at the time. (7:2) She is prepared for love described in non-metaphorical terms in the proceeding verses. Then suddenly she realizes that her lover is missing. Is it his day off? Is he sleeping off a royal party from the night before? Do they sleep in separate rooms? Are all the neighbors privy to her love life? (I have this picture in my mind of a group of ladies twittering and tiptoeing around, making sure they didn't sneeze or drop a pan in the kitchen.)

But back to the holding pattern. The lovers are waiting for the other to be available. It probably wasn't a long wait, even though passion drove the desire for a quick reunion.

Narrative: Another lesson about *holding patterns* here is that the desire for satisfaction drives our need to have the holding pattern end quickly. There is nothing wrong or unnatural about our satisfying our basic appetites for food, sleep, comfort, fun, and sex. Still, we are not good about deferring our gratification in a culture of if it feels good, do it and do it now! We don't like to be told to wait. But this is exactly what God tells us to do. And as for the Princess of the Nile and the King of Wisdom, the waiting was worth it. In fact, their union meant more because they waited for pleasure.

Our culture dislikes pain and discomfort. So we take pills and avoid reality; we lie to ourselves. We try to make the struggle go away as soon as possible by avoidance; we escape our painful realities. We pray, Lord end it, take it away, get rid of it; it hurts too much. However, we may learn that struggling with problems strengthens us; we realize that our pain can be productive. A holding pattern can help us grow into maturity. And, too, if we rush to get through our holding pattern, we fail to learn lessons God had intended.

Principle: When we want a holding pattern to end too quickly, we may forfeit the benefits of waiting.
Perspective: Colossians 1:11 "We are praying, too, that you will be filled with His mighty, glorious strength so that you can keep going no matter what happens, always full of the joy of the Lord."
Participation: Did you rush a holding pattern that would have been more beneficial if you had waited longer? If not, did your patience pay off?

The Prophetical Books

The final section of the Old Testament books centers on prophecy. It predicted the result of God's people breaking His rules and replacing Him with human kings, always a poor substitute.

Prophecy has been defined as forth-telling and foretelling. The first has to do with what is happening today and the latter with what will happen in the future. There were three major prophets and 13 minor prophets. (It sounds like baseball leagues, doesn't it?) Isaiah, Jeremiah, and Ezekiel were major; Daniel through Malachi were minor. But no prophet has a *minor* message; each has to do with the exile of Israel or the deportation of Judah. Therefore, no Israelite could use the flimsy excuse of not being told about the pending crisis. (It was on the 6:00 Capital Nightly News, but they just turned it off or changed channels!)

The *holding patterns* of the Major and Minor prophets focused on God's people to get their act together before being deported. Note that all these *holding patterns*, except one, were self-imposed by Israel's and Judah's rejection of the one true God.

It was their action that caused His reaction. He had no choice but to react. He had to be consistent as a perfect, holy, and righteous God who, as the ultimate parent, had to follow through with disciplining His errant children. He also had to prove His love to His people by doing what was best for them, which meant holding them accountable for their choices and helping them learn from their mistakes. Within this panorama of prophecy, we will examine the *holding patterns* imposed by God upon His people, each for a particular reason and a special season.

Narrative: It begins with our parents, our teacher or Scout Master, a school counselor, or a good friend who really cares about us. They tell you to stay on the main highway of life. But we take sideroads. In our pride, stubbornness, and self-will, we don't like people telling us what we don't want to hear or telling us what we should do. So we choose not to take advice; we learn the hard way! God uses these people to help us avoid the pain and problems we could have avoided if we only had listened.

Principle: Often, God sends people into our lives in a waiting period to warn us of pending conditions.
Perspective: Proverbs 9:8-9 "But a wise man, when rebuked, will love you all the more. Teach a wise man, and he will be the wiser; teach a good man, and he will learn more."
Participation: Remember when you were waiting, and someone warned you about something? Did you heed the warning? Why or why not? What was the result?

The Major Prophets

Isaiah experienced years of dread in anticipation of his inevitable death.

Background: Isaiah was of a royal bloodline, married with two sons. He was presumably the nephew of King Amaziah. While a young man, Assyria attacked Northern Israel. Thirteen years later, Samaria fell, and the rest of the Northern Kingdom was removed. Isaiah lived under Uzziah, Jotham, Ahaz, and Hezekiah. He served as a prophet and a political and religious advisor. He was a man of the palace; it was no accident he was related to royalty. It was all part of God's unique purpose for him as a prophet to His own people. He was one of the literary giants of the Bible, comparable to Shakespeare, Milton, or Homer in some minds. He has been labeled the evangelical prophet in that he foretold the coming of Christ and had six Christmas prophecies. He wrote lyrically with the great use of figurative language to describe the situation with God and His delinquent people.

Leading examples would be describing Israel as a vineyard and Christ as a branch from the root of Jesse. He clearly foretold the events surrounding the apostasy, captivity, and the ultimate restoration of the Kingdom of Israel. Isaiah is remembered as the messianic prophet. His writing presented the most detailed forecast of the coming of Christ to deliver His people and the world. He not only spoke of God's judgment on Israel but on the nations surrounding her, many of whom God used as a means by which to carry out retribution on His people.

In the sixth chapter of his letter, Isaiah was told to declare the truth even though the people would not listen to or obey it! As a result, he did not live to see the captivity of Judah at the hands of the Babylonians but did prophesy its coming.

In a real sense, Isaiah's 66-year tenure as a prophet comprised his holding pattern; he waited his entire adult life for the inevitable judgment of God on the Southern Kingdom, the coming of Israel's Redeemer, and his own martyrdom. His holding pattern ended with his being placed between two planks and sawed in half at the hand of Hezekiah's spoiled and evil son, Manasseh, in BC 695. Nevertheless, Isaiah was one of the great prophets admitted to the New Testament Hall of Faith in Hebrews 11 and quoted 64 times in the New Testament.

Narrative: Outcomes in life are not always predictable; based on handy, dandy, quick, and easy formulas: Do this, and this will happen! Some people spend a lifetime doing things without seeing the results. Missionaries give themselves to indigenous people without a convert, movie stars keep starring in films without ever taking home an Oscar, and gamblers keep the slots going in the elusive hope of winning the jackpot. In the realm of living out our Christian faith, we keep the commands, obey the directives, live lives of love and good deeds, and yet may never know what kind of impact we have made in the lives of others. When called to do the right things without knowing the outcomes, our entire life is a holding pattern between birth and eternity.

Principle: *Holding patterns* may require that we stay the course and keep doing the right things when we have no idea if it is making a difference or not.

Perspective: Hebrews 12:2 "Keep your eyes on Jesus, our leader, and instructor. He was willing to die a shameful death on the cross because of the joy He knew would be His afterwards, and now He sits in the place of honor by the throne of God."

Participation: Have you ever persevered doing what you were supposed to but not seeing results? Why is this hard?

Did you ever have someone acknowledge and confirm that you made a difference in their life or situation?

Jeremiah was commanded never to marry.
Background: God appointed Jeremiah as a priest-prophet in a disastrous time for Judah. A contemporary of Daniel and Ezekiel, he was classified as the weeping prophet mourning over the condition of God's people who worshipped the Queen of Heaven. He was threatened, put in stocks, publically humiliated as a false prophet, thrown into a pit, and left for dead.

Additionally, unlike other prophets, he was commanded to remain single. He probably saw women he would like to have married, but God said no. (Another reason why he was called the Weeping Prophet?)

Narrative: We were not created to live in solitude or self-isolation. God made us social beings. After all, each member of the Trinity had two others to do life with. So, it is instinctive for people to want to be married and have a lifetime partner. But it doesn't always work out the way we hoped and planned. It becomes more challenging in our culture where everyone seems to have a 'we complex' and thinks something is wrong with you if you are single. The pain of never finding the right one or taking a long time to tie the knot is real. Married couples especially understand the pain of losing a mate; it's one of the *holding patterns* that hurts the most.

Principle: Many people wind up living life alone or may wait a long time to find the right person.
Perspective: Psalms 147:3 "He heals the brokenhearted, binding up their wounds."

Participation: How have you or someone you know waited for a spouse for a long time or remained unmarried? What makes either of these *holding patterns* difficult?

Ezekiel waited for 25 years for his people to learn a lesson.
Background: Ezekiel was only one of two prophets who actually lived with fellow exiles in captivity. Daniel had been in Babylon for nine years when Ezekiel arrived. He was carried away with 10,000 other Jews to Babylon in 597 BC, eleven years before Jerusalem was destroyed. (Ezekiel 33:2, 40:1) He had a wife (Ezekiel 24:15-18) and lived in Telabib (Tel-Aviv?) about 40 miles away from Fara, the traditional home of Noah, about 100 miles away from Iran, the site of the Garden of Eden, a place referred to 60 times in his book. His name means God is my strength.

Ezekiel was called into the prophetic ministry at age 30 and served for 25 years. The Assyrian capture of the Northern Kingdom was 120 years before the captivity of Judah. His prophecies began six years before and seventeen years after that tragic event.

Like Isaiah and Jeremiah, who may have been his teachers, he foretold the future restoration of Israel and the downfall of neighboring nations. He also forecasted the conversion of Jews to Christ as foretold by Paul in the New Testament book of Romans. (11:15, 25-26) The central thrust of his message is the glory of the Lord.

Visions and symbolism are characteristic of Ezekiel's writing. Perhaps the most famous is the vision of the Valley of Dry Bones. This was a prediction of the national resurrection of scattered Israel when returning to their own land in the future, ultimately under the reign of the everlasting King, the Son of

God/Son of Man. There is a Messianic theme in this book centering around his use of the term Son of Man, used 93 times. Moreover, it is the same term used for Christ, the Messiah, in Daniel 7:13 and numerous times in the Old Testament. Therefore, it infers that Ezekiel was a prototype of the Great Prophet. We need to consider his five *holding patterns*.

Holding Pattern 1 Remaining mute for a protracted period.
Holding Pattern 2 Laying in one position for 390 days.
Holding Pattern 3 Eating awful food that he hated.
Holding Pattern 4 Grieving the loss of a spouse.
Holding Pattern 5 Enduring captivity on-site while trying to keep up the deported people's sagging morale.

Narrative: Keeping up with the next-door neighbor or a rich relative usually causes us to be jealous of having what someone else has. Life is centered on the mantra, 'if only I had'; fill in the blank. But we may have a different perspective when it comes to life situations in general or holding patterns specifically. Remember, whatever holding pattern you are in, someone is in the middle of one that's even harder than yours.

Principle: Sometimes, looking at the *holding patterns* of others can put ours in perspective.
Perspective: Hebrews 12:3-4 "If you want to keep from becoming fainthearted and weary, think about His patience as sinful men did such terrible things to Him. After all, you have never yet struggled against sin and temptation until you sweat great drops of blood."
Participation: What is the hardest holding pattern you have known someone else to have gone thru? How does that compare with yours? Better or worse?

The Minor Prophets

Daniel waited for over 70 years but never returned to his home.

Background: Daniel was a co-captive with Ezekiel. He was considered a mouthpiece to the Jewish and Gentile world. He was a ruler in Babylonia, the city of gold, close to the original Garden of Eden and Babel's infamous tower. Indeed, he was physically safe there; the city was 60 miles around with walls 300 feet high, 60 feet thick, extending 35 feet below the ground with 200 towers on the wall. But the Persians used the Euphrates River, which divided the city, to gain access to it when they conquered Babylon. (So much for 60 miles of border walls!)

The surroundings weren't too shabby either; the Hanging Gardens were one of the world's seven wonders, perhaps a prototype for the Eiffel Tower or the Empire State Building. The author, whose name means God is my judge, appears five times in the book that bears his name. Daniel was a Babylonian captive considered part of the Judea aristocracy, upper-crust, upper-class types.

After passing his screen test, a sequel to appearing on The Bachelor, Daniel was singled out as the dream weaver again, not unlike his fellow CEO, Joseph. Like his Genesis counterpart, he was good-looking, and uber-intelligent, making him a perfect candidate to be a court trainee selected to learn and teach the customs and life traditions to the Jewish captives. The crash course in Babylonian culture centered on the pagan god, 'Bel,' whose name was incorporated into king's names like Belshazzar.

The most famous dream/vision is of the statue of Nebuchadnezzar. He created a golden statue of himself weighing no less than 50,000 pounds! God used both Daniel to translate the king's troublesome visions forecasting the future for both Israel and the world.

It was the symbol of the superpowers of all history through the end times and the return of Christ, who was symbolized by a mighty boulder that would smash the statue to smithereens. Daniel forecasted the end times, the Antichrist rule, the persecution of God's people, and the ultimate and eternal rule of Christ when His saints would possess the kingdom.

Daniel was promoted to one of the top three positions in the cabinet. Again like Joseph, he became the official vice-president, ruling over 120 princes. He was considered a senior statesman in Babylonia-Persia, serving under six Babylonian kings and two Persian Kings. He served from the first year of the Jew's captivity until two years after their return from captivity, some 70 years.

Like Esther, both were brought to power strategically for the Jewish people. Daniel's intellect is proven by the fact that he spoke two languages. The book's first half was written in Aramaic, and the second half was Hebrew; the first was for the Babylonian people, and the second was for the Israelis. His virtue and high morals were confirmed by resisting the social pressure to do what everyone else did on three separate occasions. First, he was asked to eat a cholesterol-loaded diet (the Babylonian Big Mac) instead of a healthy one. Then, Daniel was asked to worship a pagan god and stop praying to the true God.

There is an obvious correlation between the writings of John, the author of the Apocalypse, and Daniel's vision. Daniel is often classified as the fourth major prophet because his prophecies would occur at the end of time; the reuniting of the former Roman Empire and the coming of Christ to judge and rule the earth.

Daniel's *holding patterns* included one short one and one long one. The short holding pattern: the overnight visit to the lion's den, where the question of the hour was how long until he'd get eaten alive or get out of here? The more extended holding pattern: how long would it be before he'd get to go home? He must have been home-sick as he saw the wagons head West without him!

Narrative: Life is not defined by our problems but by how we respond to them. We often can't control the problem, but we can always take charge of how we respond. And when we practice restraint and model self-control, people notice our response.

Principle: The impact of *holding patterns* on us and others depends on our response to them.
Perspective: I Peter 3:16 "Do what is right; then if men speak against you, calling you evil names, they will become ashamed of themselves for falsely accusing you when you have only done what is good."
Participation: Did you ever make a choice that impacted someone else? Was the impact positive or negative?

Hosea waited for his unfaithful wife to return to him.
Background: The second of the Minor Prophets was God's spokesman to the Northern Kingdom. Hosea's name means the same as Joshua's; Jehovah is Salvation. He was a younger contemporary of Amos. He might have known Jonah and heard all the fish tales as a child! He declared God's warning to four kings of Judah and three kings of Israel between 787-749 BC,

serving seven kings over 30 years, the four of whom were assassinated by successors. Ten of the twelve tribes of Israel had seceded from the union 200 years before him, making the golden calf its official God replacement.

During the interim, God sent the prophets Elijah, Elisha, Jonah, and Amos. He addressed both kingdoms and the fall of Samaria. Hosea is set apart from all other prophets because he became a living metaphor. God told him to marry Gomer, a harlot, which he did. She left him and became an adulteress in the same way Israel had left her God and committed spiritual adultery. Mrs. Hosea bore three children who also became living metaphors as their names would indicate the nation's status. The first stood for Retribution, the second, No More Mercy, and the third, No Longer My People, all symbolic of God's estranged relationship with his wife, Israel. His people sealed their own fate with flirtatious affairs and spiritual infidelity with pagan nations. Yet Hosea concludes his prophecy with a promise of Jehovah's wayward bride returning to the altar and renewing her vows. Despite her sin, Hosea loved Gomer just as God loved Israel.

Narrative: We probably can't count on two hands the people we have had a falling out with who refused to accept responsibility for what happened or had no intention of making things right. They just decided to go through the rest of life mad, bitter, and unforgiving. As for us, we finally decide, after all efforts are unsuccessful, to live with semi-closure. We realize we have no control over another person's response; we are only responsible for our own.

The only residual of losing a friend may be gaining insight and wisdom to help us with future relationships. Of course, it's not how we want things to turn out, but we must often move forward and get on with our adjusted life.

Principle: Waiting for the resolution of a relationship may not end in closure but simply help us adjust to a new reality.
Perspective: Romans 12:18-19 "Don't quarrel with anyone. Be at peace with everyone, just as much as possible. Dear friends, never avenge yourselves. Leave that to God, for He has said that He will repay those who deserve it. Don't take the law into your own hands."
Participation: Describe how waiting resulted in repairing a relationship or helped you adjust to losing it.

Joel died before his predictions came true.
Background: Joel's name means the Lord is God. He is considered one of the earliest of God's messengers during the reign of Joash and possibly Uzziah, making him a contemporary with Isaiah. He served as a priest/prophet but was not a Levite. Joel's prophecy is distinctive because of the prediction of the coming of the Lord and the Holy Spirit, who would facilitate the gospel witness to the whole world. A drought and a locust invasion accompanied his writing about the day of the Lord. He told God's people "to rend their hearts, not their garments." (Joel 2:13)

This prediction in space-time history is fulfilled to the very last detail in the New Testament Book of Acts, chapter two. The Holy Spirit was antecedent to the ascension of Christ and facilitated the declaration of the gospel in all human languages through those gathered together on the day of Pentecost. Thus, the forecast of Joel becomes a reality, "All who call upon the name of the Lord shall be saved." (Joel 2:32a) Three thousand people heard the dual messages of the disciples and Peter. The first coming of Christ was precedent to the second coming. Thus, Joel's prediction in the immediate referred to the House of Israel, the Old Testament People of God, and ultimately referred to the House of Faith, the New Testament People of

God. The announcement of the second coming also included the physical appearance of Christ and the seismic disturbances in the physical world that preceded it. He also forecasts the birth of the church at Pentecost. Not surprisingly, Joel has one of the longer *holding patterns* in both testaments, from 750 BC-33 AD, the span of time between the prediction and the fulfillment. He, of course, did not live to see it! Joel is not the first or the last one to believe something and never see it in their lifetime. His message of judgment and hope in his day and the last days upon the earth was yet some 2,500 years away.

Narrative: It's not very encouraging to realize some *holding patterns* will last until we enter eternity. But the key here is to remember not how long life is on earth but how long we will live in eternity. There is a comparison. Heaven will be a place with no clocks, no watches, no tardy bells, and no calendars. And *holding patterns* in the present will suddenly seem short by comparison with a timeless eternity! I know; why doesn't it start soon? Well, it will be here before we know it!

Principle: Many *holding patterns* last beyond a lifetime and extend into eternity when we see the results.
Perspective: I Corinthians 13:12 "In the same way, we can see and understand only a little about God now, as if we were peering at His reflection in a poor mirror; but someday we are going to see Him in His completeness, face-to-face. Now all that I know is hazy and blurred, but then I will see everything clearly, just as clearly as God sees into my heart right now."
Participation: What holding pattern in your life is the hardest to explain? Why?

Amos waited for some 30 years for God's forecast of captivity to actualize.

Background: This prophet was the Old Testament version of Jimmy Carter. But instead of harvesting peanuts, he gathered fruit and tended sheep. (Amos 8:14) Not a likely candidate for prophethood. But after all, David starts out as a shepherd, and look where he wound up. There is a connection between tracking sheep and keeping track of people. At any rate, Amos, whose name meant the burden bearer, was chosen by God for a sacred assignment, a heavy burden for one new to the prophetic office. (People are even harder to shepherd than sheep.) Initially, he was a prophet to Judah, the Southern Kingdom, but was sent to the Northern Kingdom thirty years before it fell. His prophecies came in the form of visions and dreams. His career was short compared to other prophets. (BC 792-765) He was one of the few dual kingdom prophets.

The reign of Jeroboam II brought about an enlargement of the kingdom and great prosperity. Unfortunately, it also brought brazen idolatry centered on the golden calf and the worship of Baal, introduced 200 years before, incorporating many of the Canaanite abominable religious practices. His prophecy came at a time of enormous economic prosperity for the Israelites. Still, though affluent, the apostate condition of this country was evident in stealing, injustice, oppression, robbery, adultery, and murder. (It sounds like another country we're familiar with, doesn't it?) God had already sent Elijah, Elisha, and Jonah, no less, but to no avail! His people believed themselves immune from judgment based on their outward religious rituals.

He and his buddy, Hosea, were a type of tag-team telling the truth, which was rejected, especially coming from a guy who had a harlot for a wife and his buddy Amos, a guy who was a fruit vendor. Both prophets were unable to stop their country's dash for death. Amos continued his ministry after Hosea's concluded. Their message not only came to their homeland but also to their wicked neighbors whose lifestyle Israel emulated. So, along comes Amos, the fruit gatherer and sheep tender who gave Israel one more chance to clean up their act. We know the rest of the story, captivity and eventual loss of their homeland. How did he feel getting up every day and doing the same job for three decades, one he didn't want and didn't even get paid for?

Narrative: Remember the chores you had as a kid and your parents telling you that it would teach you to be hard-working and responsible as a grown-up? And that's all some of us got for doing what we were supposed to do; no allowance, just a lecture on how many things our Mom and Dad did for us. ("If you had to pay the bills around here, you'd turn the lights off!") So not all the benefits of waiting are immediate. You have to keep doing what you are told to do at home or the office and get paid later, sometimes a lot later!

Principle: *Holding patterns* may involve things we don't want to do or for which we are not compensated.
Perspective: Listen to Mark 10:29-30: "And Jesus replied, Let me assure you that no one has ever given up anything; home, brothers, sisters, mother, father, children, or property for love of me and to tell others the Good News, who won't be given back a hundred times over, homes, brothers, sisters, mothers, children, and land; with persecutions!"
Participation: Have you had to do things you didn't want to do? How did God compensate you in these situations?

Obadiah waited four years for his doom and gloom prophecy to take place.
Background: Unlike his prophet peers, Obadiah didn't prophesy to Israel but to one of her enemies, the Edomites. The

Edomites were not only enemies; they were relatives of Esau. (Not the first or last time relatives didn't get along, right?) Well, maybe his family never got over carrying a grudge...something very evident in how they treated Israel.

The Edomites refused to let the nation of Israel pass through their land and were ready to join forces with an alien army to attack them. In fact, they did this four times under four kings who reigned in Judah: Jehoram, Amaziah, Ahaz, and Zedekiah.

The only one-chapter prophet predicted that Edom would be cut off forever, but a remnant of Judah would be saved and prevail, consistent with the rest of the Major and Minor Prophets.

Within four years after the fall of Jerusalem, Edom was raided and desolate. With the ultimate destruction of Jerusalem by 70 AD, the Edomites were no longer elitist enemies. They disappeared from history as predicted by Isaiah, Jeremiah, Ezekiel, and Amos. By the way, they thought they were impregnable and invincible because they built their major city, Petra, carved out of the sides of cliffs, overlooking a very narrow stretch of land, and for the most part, was inaccessible. (But not to God!) Obadiah might have had a short prophecy, but it was spot on. He was yet another prophet who foretold the future. His name means God worshipper. He knew the God whose prophecy he proclaimed, the one his people had betrayed by worshipping idols. He unknowingly gave us insight into a holding pattern.

Narrative: The Bible talks about foul-weather friends, people who betray you. They desert you when you thought you could count on them. Tough times were made tougher by traitors. Life is tough enough without your friends turning on you. People cheer you on at the wedding, but nobody is around for the divorce. But, Christ is a friend who will be with you in every life situation and knows about being betrayed by His closest friends when He needed them most.

Principle: Our *holding patterns* often involve supposed allies who became adversaries and fail to understand and support us in the midst of a crisis.
Perspective: Psalm 41:9-10a "Even my best friend has turned against me; a man I completely trusted, how often we ate together. Lord, don't you desert me! Be gracious, Lord."
Participation: How do you handle those people who let you down? Identify a time when you felt God didn't seem to come through for you. How is that different from when your friends let you down?

Jonah waited 40 days for Ninevah to repent.
Background: Perhaps the most famous and well-known prophet, certainly one of the most interesting, is best remembered for being called to a mission impossible assignment. Jonah was a coward swallowed up by a whale-like sea creature who vomited him up on a beach and then got the king of Assyria to wear sackcloth and sit in ashes. (That's all.)

The Hebrew word used was great fish. It was quite possibly a Blue Whale with a tail about twenty-five feet in length and a heart that weighed 400 pounds. It was big enough to hold 15,000 gallons of water or, more likely, a Goliath-sized Grouper fish. It could have been 12 feet in length and some 700 pounds, capable of sucking up a man in one gulp. (And imagine the heartburn for the fish!)

Nineveh was the capital of the Assyrian Empire, established by Nimrod, Noah's grandson, a world power over about 300 years. (900-607 BC) Jonah was called to 'Nasty Nineveh,' potentially prolonging the life of a brutal and merciless military machine already in the process of exterminating Jonah's people. It ultimately did, 127 years before Assyria fell. It is essential to recognize that Jonah's ultimate obedience actually kept Assyria from taking Israel captive. God also used two plagues and a solar eclipse to bring Assyria to repentance.

Critical scholars who have rejected the writing believe it is fictional, not factual. Yet, the clearest and most significant confirmation of its historicity and authenticity is Christ Himself in Matthew 12 and Luke 11. He compared Jonah being three days in the great fish and being burped up alive to His own three days in the tomb, delivered from death.

Jonah had several *holding patterns*. First, he waited for the storm at sea to subside, which it did after he bailed. Next, a run to Joppa, a city that still exists, and a three-day walk through the entire city.

Jonah had interesting reactions to his *holding patterns*, which got him back on track with God, and subsequently, he and a wicked city survived. The only thing that didn't survive was the dying shade tree he desperately needed to protect him from the sun!

Narrative: It's human nature to overlook nine things going well and zoom in on the one thing that isn't! (Remember when you got all A's but a B in Physics, and your parents went on a tirade?) And this time, you and I would say, "What does it take to please you guys?" It comes from human perfectionism, imperfect people who cannot do everything perfectly but expect everyone else to! It is easy to overlook the good things and focus on one that isn't up to your expectations; the glass as half-empty instead of half-full!

Principle: When we are on hold, we often focus on negative things more than positive things.
Perspective: I Thessalonians 5:18 "No matter what happens, always be thankful, for this is God's will for you who belong to Christ Jesus."
Participation: Are you more of a pessimist or an optimist? Why do you think that is? What steps could you take to become more optimistic if you're pessimistic?

Micah waited for over 42 years for Judah to be taken into captivity.
Background: Micah's name, Who Is A God Like You?, is a fitting question for the focus of his prophecy. He was a contemporary of Isaiah and Hosea who served under five kings; four good and one bad. Like the three major prophets, he was a spokesperson for the Northern Kingdom (Israel) and the Southern Kingdom (Judah). His message was addressed to two capitals, Samaria and Jerusalem, respectively, from which he lived 30 miles away in the city of Gath on the Philistine border. The theme of the prophecy is sin, destruction, and the restoration of the Jews, God's chosen people.

His book is a tapestry weaving together present desolation and future glory, containing one of the most poignant Messianic prophecies in the scriptures. Here, amidst the threats of present war and retribution, he references a future peace and restoration that centers on Christ's coming, the ultimate Prince of Peace and Savior of the world. Micah was a skilled orator, a master of metaphors, a wordplay genius, and a vivid imager.

He notes that a small and little-known city, Bethlehem, would bring forth a ruler who would bring the children of Israel to their land when His rule extended to the ends of the earth. But, like their New Testament counterparts, they expected a king to deliver them immediately. So when a leader didn't come, they mistreated the people, seized their fields, and ejected women and children from their homes. Again, they chose false prophets to condone their cruel and unjust conspiracy, bribery, and corruption practices. But the same God who predicted helplessness also forecasted hope and happiness for their distant future. And make no mistake, the promises to Israel are still in place; they have not been replaced by the promises made to the contemporary people of God, the Church. Both center ultimately on Christ, who sets up His eternal kingdom where all believers from every nation will live with Him forever. (Glorious!)

Like his prophet counterparts, Micah lived in a holding pattern waiting for the bomb to drop; for the promised judgment to fall on both halves of the divided kingdom. But, being a prophet, called to bring bad news, his was a lonely occupation for which few resumes were submitted!

Imagine the editorial in the Jerusalem Journal would read: Prophet wanted. Some fortune-telling experience is required. Camel hair uniform provided, minimum wage with no benefits except meeting royalty who may dislike and kill you after hearing your presentation. (You wouldn't have to interview more than one applicant if you even had one!) But, those who signed on simply told people what they wanted to hear, even if it was false!

Narrative: In life, we like people to solve our problems. We tend to want others to tell us what we *want* to hear rather than what we *ought* to hear! Easy answers often make us feel good and comfortable but cause us to avoid confronting reality and dealing with the needed changes. They make life easy at the moment but not so easy later when we have to face the truth and do what it requires. Note to self: Go to people who love and care enough to level with you. These people are the same ones who will be your true friends and still be there to face and work through the challenges with you!

Principle: When we go through *holding patterns*, people will always try to give us easy answers to complex questions, telling us God's plan for our lives.
Perspective: Deuteronomy 18:21-22 "If you wonder, how shall we know whether the prophecy is from the Lord or not? This is the way to know: If the thing he prophesies doesn't happen, it is not the Lord who has given him the message; he has made it up himself. You have nothing to fear from him."
Participation: Have you known someone who seemed to have all the answers to the questions you faced or attempted to play God in your life? How did or do you handle these people?

Nahum lived all his life with the uncertainty of surviving.
Background: Nahum is the last of three prophets whose prophecy was directed to a specific city, Ninevah. Obadiah and Jonah were the other two prophets. His name means comfort/consolation, a part of the city name, Capernaum, which later became the center of Christ's ministry. He was from Elkosh, a nearby city about 20 miles north of Ninevah. Nahum came about 150 years after Jonah (785 BC), the latter a message of mercy; the former a message of doom. He was also a contemporary of Zephaniah, who predicted the downfall of Ninevah. (Zephaniah 2:13-15) He was called to bring the second warning of impending judgment; God had given the Assyrian people a chance to make a U-turn. They did, but then started down the old road again. Within 20 years of the prediction, it was fulfilled through a takeover by the Babylonians. The bloody, vile city passed into oblivion. Like another city, Tyre, it was as if it had never existed. By the way,

the Jewish captives from both kingdoms could have actually met their ancestors from Assyria in Babylonia. (It's a small world, after all!)

Nahum was anything but ho-hum! His warnings were obviously short and to the point. He said all he needed to say in 47 verses covering 28 years! He could not have encapsulated it more succinctly: A city that forgets God has a not-so-good ending. He used a form of psychological warfare against the savage Assyrians, taunting them for their dependency on false gods and human military powers instead of turning to the true God and His superhuman resources.

We need to look at Nahum's *holding patterns* from a dual perspective; childhood and adulthood. As a child living 20 miles down the road (about a two-day walk) from a capitol city of power, he lived with the inevitability of attack. (It was a little like living close to Berlin in the 1940s.) As an adult, he lived with the certainty of God's judgment on and destruction of the same city and the Assyrian Kingdom. His people had gone into captivity, assimilating into other lands and with other peoples. He was a descendant of Israeli captives taken by Assyrians in 722 BC; thus, his *holding patterns* were in unfamiliar surroundings. He waited in strange circumstances which had little promise of ever changing.

Narrative: Have you ever felt awkward in a situation you wound up in but couldn't change? When this happens, we look at how things are going and wish we could change the direction. But we live life relying on the weather forecast to assure that the family reunion picnic is still on or the stock market index is up. Our focus is on variable temporary happiness rather than the eternal God who never changes in the world where everything else does!

Principle: *Holding patterns* may put us in unusual circumstances. We may feel uncomfortable, yet we learn to trust.
Perspective: "I am, the Lord, I do not change." Malachi 3:6a
Participation: Was there a time in your life when you found yourself in strange, uncomfortable circumstances? Was it hard to trust in God? If so, did you trust in other things instead? Name them.

Zephaniah waited 31 years to see God's enemies destroyed.
Background: Zephaniah was of royal lineage along with Isaiah and Daniel. It was a terrible time for the Southern Kingdom, already headed for the cliff. But the trip to the edge was slowed down by the boy-king who began his rule at age eight, the great-grandson of Hezekiah, another good king.

Zephaniah ties with Hosea for the longest minor prophet writing, 14 chapters to be exact. Hosea's theme was an unfaithful Israel; Zephaniah's theme was doomsday for Judah. It's a sad narrative. God's holy and set-apart people allowed themselves to be lumped together with other godless nations who worshiped Baal and Molech. They were to live contrasting lives, bearing witness of the only true and living God, the Lord Jehovah, but they blew that! However, having a good king for a change made Zephaniah's job much easier compared to Isaiah, Jeremiah, Ezekiel, and nearly all the rest of the Minor Prophets who served under big-time evil rulers. Yet, instead of learning from their mistakes, God's people repeated them!

This is why Zephaniah's book centers in the Great Day of God, mentioned eleven times in the first three chapters. It has two different meanings; it had to do with two different days. The first would be a sad day for Israel and the surrounding nations, and the whole world. Then, in the last chapter of the writing, it becomes a glad day on which the remnant nation of Israel returns from centuries of bondage and dispersion. Their universal witness to the world will be to all nations who will come to salvation, Jews from the nation of Israel and Gentiles from neighboring nations. Their disobedience forfeited the opportunity to carry out their mission.

Imagine watching their punishment happen, knowing it could have been avoided. It has been said that those who fail to learn from history are doomed to repeat it. Unfortunately, Israel had a long history of failure, which they chose to perpetuate.

Narrative: It's hard to accept that sometimes a holding pattern doesn't make us euphoric or ecstatic. It makes us examine how we live, make better choices, and go in a different direction. They are not the things you can talk about, like how much you made on the sale of your home, your next trans-Atlantic trip, or a new wardrobe; nothing character-producing. Instead, it is something noticeable; maybe just slight changes, a wiser and improved you, focusing on things that matter and have lasting value.

Principle *Holding patterns* teach us about errors in our life we hopefully won't repeat.
Perspective: Exodus 34:9 "And he said, if it is true that I have favor in your sight, O Lord, then please go with us to the Promised Land, yet, it is an unruly, stubborn people, but pardon our iniquity and our sins, and accept us as your own."
Participation: Is there a habit or a pattern of behavior you've repeated that you could have avoided? How did overcoming a bad behavior develop a positive character quality in you?

Habbakuk became impatient with God for not making good on His promise.

Background: His name meant to embrace, implying that he could finally embrace God's promise as fulfilled on God's timetable, not his own. His career began with the death of Josiah, one of the few good kings of Judah. He expresses his concern about God using Babylon as a tool of judgment on His people. Habbakuk is famous for his pronouncement that "the just shall live by faith," which God had to teach him through a life experience.

His thrust is on the character and sovereignty of God Himself and the ultimate Savior He would send many generations later, at the perfect time. He pronounces judgment against Juhah for her sins for which they will be destroyed; markets, merchants, wealth, houses, and vineyards. But he also announces judgments on the kingdoms God will use to carry it out; Philistia, Moab, Ammon, Cush, and Assyria.

Finally, amid the destruction of the present, he forecasts the deliverance of the future when God's governance and worship will be re-instated. But unfortunately, this impatient prophet saw that God did not perform as he thought he should, something his fellow Israelites no doubt noticed and emulated.

Narrative: We're always in a hurry in a 'Grab and Go' culture. We want it now, but we still hurry and wait for Target to open on Black Friday. But we don't like being on hold.

My wife and I are polarized when it comes to patience. She confessed that she pre-opened the gifts in the early years of our marriage and re-wrapped them before Christmas. It took me six years to figure that out! By thy way, I now bring out all her gifts at the last minute! I contend that anticipation is a big deal for me; I love looking forward to a surprise. It makes the gifts even more special because my waiting is rewarded.

Principle: When we are impatient to see things happen too quickly in our *holding patterns*, we may miss its benefits.
Perspective: Proverbs19:2 "It is dangerous and sinful to rush into the unknown."
Participation: Do you have a childhood memory of wanting something to happen right away? Have you had any occurrences in adulthood like that? Did you learn anything about yourself in these circumstances?

Haggai waited 14 years to complete the rebuilding of the temple.
Background: This prophet's name means Festal, a person born on a Feast Day, one of many days set apart to celebrate what God had done. Haggai returned from captivity under Zerubbabel with 55,000 other Jews to rebuild the city, the first cause of celebration.

Haggai was one of three prophets, along with Zechariah and Malachi, who lived in the period after the captivity. This period, which we are told about in the books of Ezra and Esther at the close of Old Testament history, covers about 100 years from 536-432 BC. The period was divided into two parts. The first was under the leadership of Governor Zerubbabel during the time the temple was rebuilt. The second was under the leadership of Governor Nehemiah and the priest Ezra, who rebuilt the walls to fortify the city of Jerusalem.

The thrust of his message was the temple. The first was the old one built by Solomon. Then, Zechariah and the people built the new one. Finally, the eternal temple would be built by Christ at the end of the age.

The writing was two-fold; one to get the people to renew the building effort that had stalled. Two, to put as much into making the temple beautiful as they did their own opulent houses. In the opening verses of the first chapter, he asks this question, "Is it time for you yourselves to be living in your paneled houses while this house remains a ruin?" Haggai 1:4 (NIV)

The real issues were more than stopping by the Hebrew Home Depot to get supplies; it was the people getting off their duffs and doing something. It also reminded people not to be casual and complacent about the house of God, the center of religious worship, and not become consumed with themselves and their comforts. (Wouldn't ya' think they would have remembered that after going into captivity?) Instead, these people suffered a not-so-rare form of spiritual amnesia! And when they forgot God, He sent them a crop failure to remind them of their failure to deal with the temple dilemma.

Although diplomatic in his directness, you can pick up a bit of disgust in Haggai. His question infers a commandment. So within 24 workdays, the old foundations had been cleared away to sufficiently reveal the outline of a new temple, which was a dwarf compared to the first one. The old-timers were immediately upset over how plain it was. For the Jews old enough to remember Solomon's temple, Haggai's temple looked more like a pup tent than a palace-like pavilion. To the younger generation, it was the most magnificent temple they had ever seen, having nothing to compare it with.

This is why it was so crucial for Haggai to bring up the third temple, the one yet to come at the end of the world, the beginning of eternity. Haggai had to play the role of a prophet and historian, contractor, cheerleader, consoler, and optimist. (A multi-tasking prophet for sure!) All three groups of people had to be excited about God doing something bigger beyond what they could see at the moment.

Narrative: Have you ever worked a jigsaw puzzle and lost the lid to the box? It is much harder to put the pieces together! Why? Because you forget what the puzzle is supposed to look like. Life is a puzzle. (10,000 pieces at least, right?) The problem is that we are overwhelmed by the number of pieces, but we have little or no idea of what the whole thing, put together, is supposed to look like. God's will and purpose for the world and our lives are like that. To use another metaphor, God looks at the forest; we only see a single tree. God knows we are human and limited in how we see things, but we need to look at life from His perspective, the eternal over the immediate.

Principle: *Holding patterns* can be less productive if we fail to focus on the bigger picture of what God is trying to do.
Perspective: Ephesians 3:20 "Now glory be to God, who by His mighty power at work within us is able to do far more than we would ever dare to ask or even dream of, infinitely beyond our highest prayers, desires, thoughts or hopes."
Participation: Describe when you focused on a piece rather than the whole puzzle. What eventually was the bigger picture that you might have seen retrospectively?

Malachi waited 400 years to witness the fulfillment of the last prophecy.
Background: Malachi, whose name means the Lord's Messenger, was the last prophet in the Old Testament. He was a member of the Great Synagogue, which collected and preserved the scriptures. A remnant had returned from captivity (536 BC) and re-built the temple and the walls. Captivity had cured their idolatry, but they were yet prone to

neglect the House of God; even the priests had become lax and degenerate, and their required sacrifices were inferior.

His sermon contained six points: Forbidden mixed marriages, withholding of tithes, social injustice, violation of Sabbath rest, unlawful divorce, and outward religious ritual. All these issues are addressed in four brief but blunt chapters. Finally, he gives the final prophetic message of the Old Testament. His people had not only sinned but failed God in carrying out His mission to the world. Embarrassed by their self-caused deportment, they settled comfortably in a stagnant state, again lacking the incentive to change. They had regressed big time. In a sense, they had divorced themselves from God spiritually, and God states that divorce is something He hated. (Malachi 2:16)

Yet, their only hope was waiting for their Messiah to come. Instead, they were faced with mixed emotions. They would be restored but judged, forgiven but held accountable. Thus, they lacked the assurance of a personal relationship with God, whom they would come to know through the redemption of Christ.

Malachi had two long-term *holding patterns* in his life. The first was a 55-year span as he waited for the returned captives to reform themselves; it was the last call for world repentance before the final judgment.

There is no assurance that this ever happened in his life. This is documented because Israel would cease to be a formidable power globally. She would be forced into submission to foreign powers for the next 19 centuries before the budding of the fig tree, which indicated the re-gathering of Jews in their homeland and the second coming of the long-awaited Messiah, who would reclaim them as His people.

The second holding pattern for Malachi and the people was the 400 years of silence during which there would be no more prophets to speak words of warning, comfort, or hope; not until a young man, the cousin of Jesus, appeared would there be a divine messenger. Then, John the Baptist would finally break the silence in a period sequel to Israel's four hundred years in Egypt as the forerunner of Christ.

As we reflect on the last prophet's holding pattern, we see how commonplace it is for human beings to become so overwhelmed with their guilt and failure that they give up on themselves, lose perspective, and the hope that they are even salvageable. God's unfaithful people doubted that anyone, especially God, would love them or consider them worthy of being forgiven.

At the end of one of the longest *holding patterns* in human history, the prophet promises that God would send His Son to love, forgive, redeem, and restore our relationship with God Himself. He would give abundant life in the present and hope in the future. He who came the first time to *save* lives will return the second time to *reign* in the lives of those who He saves.

Narrative: At any stage in life, a holding pattern of an incredible length can engulf us, cause us to second guess ourselves, and struggle with our security and identity. It causes us to question our abilities, punish ourselves for failing and carry guilt for things we have done or should have done. All of this makes what seems like a never-ending time-out especially painful. It is compounded by our enemy's attack to undermine our faith in God, who delivers us from our dilemma. Yet, He is present; He sees, knows, and cares about everything happening to us. Never is being rescued more significant than going underwater for the third time. When we are at worst, He is at His best. The 'Eternal Life Guard' is in His heavenly lookout, ready and able to retrieve us from the raging sea of sin and its deadly consequences and bring us to permanent safety.

Principle: Often, in our *holding patterns,* we may feel overwhelmed, hopeless, and unloved, making us more desperate for deliverance from our dilemma.
Perspective: Psalm 147:11 "But His joy is in those who reverence Him, those who expect Him to be loving and kind."
Participation: Have you ever felt overwhelmed, hopeless, unloved, or desperate in your holding pattern? Did you come to see God differently in this time of waiting? How?

THE NEW TESTAMENT

Preface

The *holding patterns* of the Old Testament differ from the New Testament in several ways:

1. The Old Testament patterns had a specific duration; they were finite and ended in a certain amount of time. The New Testament patterns were more inclined to be infinite, not limited to a specific amount of time.

2. Unlike the Old Testament, which features a vast array of individuals, the New Testament centers on only a few people: Christ, His family, His church, His apostles, and His disciples.

3. It points to a life beyond this one, an eternal life, which will constitute the longest holding pattern of all, one that never ends. Why? Because all the things we have waited for during our *holding patterns* will be actualized.

We will take an up-close and personal look at the life of Christ and those in His sphere of influence and how *holding patterns* impacted their lives.

One thing worth noting; even though the New Testament people lived in a time closer to the consummation of the present age and the coming of Christ, they had the same struggles waiting out their *holding patterns*.

The Gospels

Matthew

Mary and Joseph waited a lifetime, unsure of the destiny of their son's life. (Chapters I and 2)

Background: The earthly foster parents of Christ were common folk chosen for an uncommon assignment, one that would change BC to AD. Joseph's family line was linked to Abraham (Matthew 1) and Adam (Luke 3) to underscore His Messianic lineage.

It was not a last-minute decision by God to choose Joseph to be His son's earthly father. Yet, we don't know a lot about these two people. We know Joseph was considerably older than Mary, who was related to Elizabeth, the mother of John the Baptist. Mary was most likely a teenager when he married her. It certainly was an arranged marriage by God; something usually left to parents to orchestrate in ancient cultures.

We are quite certain of two things, however. First, they loved each other and were godly individuals; they were no strangers to waiting. There was a custom of betrothal in biblical times, the term from which we get the language of traditional wedding vows. ("Hereby I pledge thee my troth.")

The betrothal period was one year when the couple was officially engaged but not actually married; they were to refrain from sexual relations. It was a holding pattern during which Mary and Joseph remained abstinent. This explains why Joseph was so embarrassed and fearful of reactions to the pregnancy and why Mary was startled by the prediction that she would be pregnant since she knew not a man. The biblical word intercourse is to know someone intimately; the modern euphemism is to sleep with someone. These two virgins had done neither.

Looking at this holding pattern more closely, we will see it extended longer than nine months. The couple would live with a perceived social stigma of having a child out of wedlock. Sure, some would ultimately recognize that the child was of divine conception, but that took a while. (God was the father, but how believable was that?) You get the picture. Yet, Mary and Joseph went on to have at least five of their own children.

The second holding pattern involved their son, God's son, growing up. How long would it be before He would start acting Messiah-like? Commentators postulate that Christ freed endangered animals in His boyhood, settled conflicts between peers, or dramatically called fire from heaven to eradicate the bully on the playground. He, in fact, learned a trade, becoming a carpenter's apprentice. Supposedly, not until He came into puberty did he show forth His divine attributes demonstrably while teaching in the temple, without a degree in theology or attending Pharisee School. Scripture records that He was about His Father's business and wasn't building houses for the Galilean Habitat for Humanity!

But when Mary and Joseph realized their earthly son had a divine mission, they had to wonder. "Is this the way it will be for the rest of His life?" How long would the holding pattern be? When the earthly parents of Christ took Him to the temple on the eighth day of His life, they heard two amazing prophecies, which may have increased their tentativeness. Mary was perhaps more anxious as she processed this child's dedication. Given the age of Joseph, it would cause her to worry about becoming a widow prematurely and not have the help and assistance of her eldest son in the carpentry business.

Then, the Roman-appointed monarch, Herod, instructed the astrologers, "Let me know where the Christ is so I can come and worship Him." (Right, Herod, worship, and murder sound so much alike!) After the visitors avoided Herod, he killed all the boy babies under two to eliminate any kingly competition.

One night Joseph and Mary were instructed by an angelic messenger to take the child to Egypt, as predicted by the Minor Prophet, Hosea. (Hosea 1:11) God appeared to Joseph a second time in a dream to instruct him on how to care for the young Christ. The human parents of Jesus were to remain in Egypt until Herod was dead at the age of 69. We do not know how long Christ was with His family in Egypt. The next time we read about Him is in the temple at age 12, then as a grown man entering His three-plus years of ministry with His second cousin John the Baptist.

It is noteworthy that He did not return to live in Jerusalem, the metropolis of its day, but to Nazareth, Galilee. His ministry was to a commoner rather than the political elite. Another holding pattern occurred when the three of them waited for Herod to die while in Egypt, not the most Jew-friendly place on the planet. After all, the Egyptians had bad memories of enslaved people, plagues, and drowned armies!

Yet, the most challenging holding pattern was the one that began when Christ entered the last three years of His adult life to complete His heavenly Father's mission. It was not about whether awful things would happen but when they would happen. Unfortunately, historical scholars cannot clearly determine if Joseph was still alive in the later years. Some believe he may have preceded Mary in death before the crucifixion. Why else would Christ assign the care of His mother to His beloved apostle, John?

The long wait for the end of His earthly mission and all its glorious implications for the whole of humanity brought sorrow and remorse to Mary. She saw Him die a brutal death as an innocent victim, one hated for being and doing good, unlike anything the world had ever seen. Yet, she knew that His death would be only temporary and that they would see Him again at the end of the world, which would be an even longer holding pattern.

Narrative: Some of you know exactly how that feels. You know what it is like to lose a child prematurely long before they reach adulthood, are miscarried or stillborn, or die within hours of birth. Others have lived with the reality of abuse who were victims in an emotional Egypt. Others see their dreams for their child evaporate. Ask the parent whose child became a nun or missionary or felt called to work with impoverished, sick people in a foreign country. Parents, especially mothers, know the feeling of loss, whether the child takes the high road or the low road. Mary, one of the greatest women and mothers of all time, knew genuine losses. These were not wholly compensated by the highest humanitarian act of redemption her Son completed for all the world. It was a holding pattern she had to live through every day of her life.

Few of us are fortune tellers. We may have a vague sense of what's coming. It's obvious it will be torrid in Texas in August, but we don't know how high the temperatures will be or if it will rain on our wedding day! But we do know some things; our eyes won't change color, we will get old, and we will die unless Christ comes back first. Some of us learn the lesson to make the best of the situation without expecting to understand or explain everything. Others of us want to know everything and try to control it. But, of course, if that were the case, many of us would still be in bed! Or, to put it another way. If I had to tell you how electricity works, we'd both be in the dark most of the time!

Principle: Times of waiting find us in circumstances we can't change at the time.
Perspective: I Peter 1:8-9 "You love Him even though you have never seen Him, though not seeing Him, you trust Him, and

even now you are happy with the inexpressible joy that comes from heaven itself. And your further reward for trusting Him will be the salvation of your souls."

Participation: How do we keep going through a holding pattern that seems to be endless, which we can't explain or control?

The Wisemen did not know where they were going or how long it would take to get there. (Matthew 2:1-2)

Background: These unusual men were a highly significant part of the confirmation of the coming of Christ as an infant. They were considered non-Jews and thus unlikely to know or be interested in a Jewish Messiah! Moreover, these men were from Babylonia, the nation that had taken the Kingdom of Judah into captivity, the cradle of civilization. It was the place where the human race began!

One thing classifies these wise guys; they were astronomers, not astrologers; they studied the stars but did not guide their lives by them. However, by studying the stars, they were guided to make a very specific trip at an exact time to a precise location.

They saw a most unusual star, one believed to interconnect two planets, Jupiter and Saturn. Is it any surprise that the One who made the heavenly bodies could align them at just the right time? This sighting took place about 6 BC, which computes with the actual birth date of Christ in 4 BC. It also makes sense because the length of the trip was about two years, judging from the age of the Christ child when the wise men first saw Him and His parents in their home before they escaped to Egypt.

Secondly, the king's advisors were amongst the Babylonian elite, thus having access to Herod, who received them as credible spokespersons with a message about Messiah. Seemingly, God prompted them to begin their arduous journey two years after the actual birth. In this way, they would arrive on the scene at just the right time.

There were most likely more than three. We assume the number three because of the three gifts; gold, frankincense, and myrrh. In addition, there could have been many wise men, also called seers, who gave the king guidance. Daniel did it when he translated the dreams for Nebuchadnezzar's statue and the writing on the wall for Belshazzar. So they created quite a stir in King David's royal city, riding in on their camels with glamourous gifts.

Interestingly, their arrival confirmed that Christ was alive and well at age two. And their gifts provided enough capital for the family's trip to Egypt, something hard to have on a carpenter's salary. The holding pattern is obvious. It was at least two years long. Think of it; a group of stargazers leaves the comfort of Babylon to make a 1000-mile trip by camel to follow an unusual star which took them to an infant monarch, whom they didn't believe in.

You talk about walking by faith. This is a classic example. And we're not talking about the Jewish patriarchs; we are talking about a bunch of Babylonian prognosticators.

Narrative: And so you are asking what can we learn from a holding pattern in the lives of these wisemen? We learn several things. When you are motivated by a mission, you can stay the course and reach your ultimate destination.

When facing a challenge, we often say, "That's impossible!" You run a marathon? The house you've always wanted going on the market? You being promoted to vice-president of the company? Not in this lifetime! So we have one of two choices: Either give up on our dreams or trust God to surprise us, only something our impossibility specialist can do!

Principle: A holding pattern can require us to do something impossible without intervention from a power beyond ourselves.

Perspective: Romans 4:20-21 "But Abraham never doubted. He believed God, for his faith and trust grew ever stronger, and he praised God for this blessing even before it happened. He was completely sure that God was well able to do everything he promised."

Participation: Record one or more times when you were in the exact place you belonged, knowing that only the Lord could make your dream happen. How did it change you?

Luke

Anna waited a lifetime to fulfill her life's purpose. (Luke 2:36-38)

Background: Anna is one of the few women mentioned in the New Testament in relation to the birth of Christ, along with His mother, Mary, and aunt Elizabeth. Her role is unique in that she is a prophetess, a foreteller of the future. She belongs to another group of women, each a prophetess; Miriam, Deborah, Huldah, and Hannah.

There is a correlation between the two women. Hannah was the mother of Samuel, the first priest-prophet of the Old Testament who served in the temple, and Anna, who served as a resident prophet in the temple. She was given a designated chamber and considered a temple-sweeper, one who trimmed the lamps lighted for worship. Thus, she was a woman of honor in the religious system of that day.

After the destruction of the remaining tribes of Israel and the dispersion of her people, ancestral connections were disregarded. Anna, however, had traced her lineage as coming out of Asher, one of the twelve sons of Jacob.

At about age 15, she married, then lost her husband after only seven years, and was widowed. Her tenure of service in the temple was about 62 years, during which she never left the temple but worshipped day and night with fasting and prayer. Like a first-century nun, she cloistered herself from the outside world. It was as if she became married to the Lord to compensate for the loss of her husband after such a short time. Her devotion to the Lord and her attending service in the temple qualified her to be the one who would prophesy concerning His coming to her people who looked forward to the redemption of Jerusalem.

One can hardly fathom the sheer joy of this moment when Mary and Joseph brought their infant son to the temple to be circumcised. This allowed the prophet Simeon, and Anna, a prophetess, to see the Christ child with their own eyes before they died.

Imagine waiting, praying, and prophesying for 62 years, never thinking that you would see the holy prediction come true, then suddenly surprised by its fulfillment. This was something that was pre-determined by divine design to happen before time. Anna was the first of many eye-witnesses to confirm the coming Savior in space-time history. She held God incarnate in her frail arms. Perhaps all that had happened in her tragic, lonely life was to prepare her for this moment; one of the greatest moments in her life and the life of the world.

Narrative: We usually come to appreciate our most extended *holding patterns* with 20/20 hindsight. We see good things that came from it that we didn't know at the time. A note we write, a kind deed we do, a friend in trouble we help; things that can occur as we persevere through life year after year. Someone is always helped by our life even when we mess up and fall short; no experience is ever wasted. What we go thru, we learn for two. Everything counts for something and someone.

Principle: Our longest *holding patterns* can sometimes work out to be the most beneficial for ourselves and others.
Perspective: II Corinthians 4:17-18 "These troubles and sufferings of ours are, after all, quite small and won't last very long. Yet this short time of distress will result in God's richest blessing upon us forever and ever!"
Participation: What has been your most extended holding pattern? Perhaps you are still in it. Identify someone who helped you through your holding pattern. Is there someone you may have helped?

Christ's Earthly Ministry
We focus now on the *holding patterns* in the life of the Lord, all of which are a part of His earthly ministry as the God-Man, the Word made flesh, who dwelt among us.

Preparation for Ministry (Matthew 3)
Background: Four hundred years had passed since Israel's God had spoken. The writer of the book of Hebrews put it this way, "God who spoke to His people in many different ways including the prophets has spoken in these last times by His Son." (Hebrews 1:1-2)

All of the Old Testament centered and pointed to this cataclysmic moment, the coming of the Messiah, the firstborn baby boy who would be murdered as a man for the sins of the world. Thus, the whole of the New Testament recorded the fulfillment of the prediction of the life and ministry of Christ.

After some 400 years of waiting, Christ appears. After only 30 years of maturation, He began doing His heavenly Father's work, which was pre-ordained and assigned to Him. Jesus experienced three major *holding patterns* in His life from birth to death. Thirty years of *preparation*, three years of *activation*, and three days of *culmination*.

In the opening chapters of the first Gospel recorded by Matthew, a converted tax collector, we witness the first scene of the world's greatest production, the preparation of Christ for His ministry of bringing salvation to a fallen planet.

As a groomsman attending to the need of the groom, Christ's cousin, John the Baptist, preceded Him. Malachi's last Old Testament prophet alluded to this renegade New Testament prophet who would be unconventional in appearance and presentation and irked the religious leaders. (Of course, it didn't take much!) John was the opening act before Christ, the big headliner who showed up, the One everybody really wanted to see.

John the Baptist preached the message of turning your life around and getting right with God, but his altar calls produced few adherents to this wild man in funny clothes with an offensive message.

He entered into the life and ministry of Christ. He would baptize the Savior, the act which would symbolize one's identity with Christ until the end of time. He would also experience an ah-ha moment in which God, the Father, would open heaven as He would do 14 chapters later when God confirmed His Son to be who He claimed to be. But, first, John was in a holding pattern anticipating his own calling as the forerunner and way maker for Christ.

I can only imagine what was running thru John's mind as he waited. Would Christ actually show up? Would he have to leave his own ministry and lose his own followers? What would happen to him when he confirmed Christ as his successor? So many questions, ones without answers.

After the wedding, the role of the groomsman changes; his services are no longer needed; thank you very much! When the star steps on the stage, the opening act exits. John graciously stepped aside to make way for Christ. He encouraged his followers to follow Christ. We also know that John had doubts about Jesus later, even after the grand opening. Christ's ministry was radically different from what he and his followers expected it to be.

Narrative: Our life can be a holding pattern, often a means to an end, to pave the way for others. A parent sacrifices to send a kid to college who becomes a Pultizer Prize Chemist but never includes them in the credits at the awards ceremony. A mother works three jobs to see that her son gets into Medical School but never gets her own GED. Grandparents who choose to raise their own grandchildren feel taken for granted and go on with the task without thanks.

Principle: In our *holding patterns*, we may help someone without getting the credit or reward for what is accomplished.
Perspective: John 3:29-30 "The crowds will naturally go to the main attraction, the bride will go where the bridegroom is! A bridegroom's friends rejoice with him. I am the Bridegroom's friend, and I am filled with joy at his success. He must become greater and greater, and I must become less and less."

Participation: Did you ever play a role in making someone else great? How were you rewarded, or were you?

The Temptation (Matthew 4)

Background: Forty was a number that had significance in the scripture; Noah endured the worldwide flood for 40 days. Moses survived wandering in the wilderness for 40 years. Before Christ was prepared to enter His momentous ministry, He had to enter 40 days of intensive testing. Satan tested Christ at this critical encounter. The ledge where this took place is still visible in a rock quarry near Jericho. It is noteworthy that the Holy Spirit led Christ into the wilderness. The run-in with Satan was not a spur-of-the-moment decision or a last-minute change of strategy. It was on God's agenda from before time.

It is important to understand the difference between testing and tempting; they are different words in the scriptures. The difference can be defined in another way; God tests us to bring out the best; Satan tempts us to bring out the worst.

The temptation was to bring out the best in Christ. However, God knew the outcome because His Son, now human, would have to be totally dependent on God His Father to get through it.

And it was not a small test. The Devil offered temporary things in place of eternal ones. He deduced that Jesus could be tempted to forfeit the most critical objective, acquiring salvation for the whole of humanity. So he tested His commitment to doing what was best for us in the long term versus what was best for Himself in the short term. And Christ was vulnerable to failing the test. He had only been on the job for a few days, maybe weeks, and hadn't eaten for 40 days. So the first of the three tests from the adversary of His soul was to get Christ to change stones into what else, bread? After all, the diabolical one knew Jesus would and could turn water into wine, so why not stones into bread? Note that though Christ was the Son of God, He was also the Son of Man; He was fully human and could become tired and hungry.

Satan used tailor-made temptations perfectly suited to his victim's vulnerabilities. Christ knew if He flunked this test, He would mess up the rest of His mission. An impulsive selfish decision could circumvent the destiny of giving His life for the sins of the world. He also could not afford to fail this test because there would be many more to come. The scriptures indicate that Satan failed to get Christ to disobey in the wilderness but would return at a more convenient time, perhaps a better time to get Christ to foul up and fail the test. But that strategy never worked. Why? Because Christ never failed the temptation test. He used tailor-made truths of scripture to resist temptation and overcome sin.

This holding pattern illustrates one from the Old Testament when Abraham was asked to offer his chosen son Issac as a human sacrifice. Although short, both holding patterns in the Old and New Testaments were very intensive. And remember, it was through the ancestry of Isaac, the one not sacrificed, that Christ, the perfect sacrifice atoned for the world's sin.

Narrative: We live in a society obsessed with the present. We often do what feels good and selfishly compromise the welfare of others for our own interests. We do something at the moment without considering the impact of our actions on the future. When we put the needs of others above our own, God will make sure we get what we need. When we don't, our needs aren't met, and the needs of others may be neglected as a result of our selfishness.

Principle: We are more inclined to focus on immediate gratification than what is ultimately important during a holding pattern.

Perspective: Phillippians 2:4-6 "Don't just think about your own affairs, but be interested in others, too, and in what they are doing. Your attitude should be the kind that was shown us by Jesus Christ, who, though He was God, did not demand and cling to His rights as God."

Participation: Did you ever put immediate self-gratification above considering your life or the lives of others? Do you regret that now? Why or Why not?

A Girl and a Woman (Mark 5:22-34)

Background: This snapshot of Christ's earthly ministry is of two women for whom the number 12 is significant. An older woman had a bleeding condition for 12 years, and a young girl had died who was only 12 years old.

Their healings are interrelated because the little girl died while Christ was healing the woman. But, the first divine delay in Christ's ministry allowed God's power to be more clearly evident.

The woman had spent all her money on physicians who probably sent her home with the newest medication without getting to the cause of her problem. She had heard about Jesus and His miracles. She needed a miracle; she was desperate, having bled every day for twelve years.

So she took a risk. She may have thought there was something magical in the Messiah's clothing, but it took genuine faith and a lot of nerve to think that if you could touch someone's garment, you would be healed! (And for a woman, no less!) What was she thinking? No doubt, she asks herself if she was doing something without permission. Was she stealing something that didn't belong to her? Would He call her down in public, or worse, would He punish her? None of this happened. She was healed; Christ even complimented her faith and told her to go in peace, which she no doubt did in a hurry with no more bleeding! The Great Physician had succeeded where all others had failed, and He did it for free!

The girl, a pre-teen, had just begun her life. There is no indication that a fortune had been spent on doctors, although her father was a synagogue ruler who could probably have afforded it. He was part of the synagogue leadership is both interesting and significant. The Jewish leaders didn't care, and they actually hated Jesus personally. But they seemed to have faith enough to take advantage of His supernatural powers. Christ went to the home where professional paid mourners attempted to divert attention from the death by wailing and putting on a sideshow. Finally, Christ said, "She is sleeping, and I will wake her up." One person was sick and made well. The other was dead and was made alive!

Narrative: *Holding patterns* come to people of all ages, early and late in life. At both ends of the spectrum, we find ourselves waiting. Usually, the *holding patterns* for children are more challenging because they have little sense of time and can grow impatient more easily. They wait for different things, a trip to the circus, a sleepover, a call back from someone they have a crush on. *Holding patterns* for adults are potentially impacted by the reality that waiting is commonplace in life. They hope for more complex things; a diagnosis from the doctor, if their health insurance premium goes up, or what to do when facing life alone after 60 years of marriage. At any age, *holding patterns* seem like a matter of life and death, no matter how they compare to everyone else's.

Principle: *Holding patterns* come to us at all ages and all stages of life. Time and experience may help us respond to the wait differently than earlier in life.
Perspective: Luke 1:37 "For every promise from God shall surely come true."
Participation: Identify the difference between how you responded to waiting when you were younger compared to the stage of life in which you find yourself now.

A Hungry Crowd (Mark 8:1-13, John 6:4-14)
Background: There were actually two hungry crowds. One is made up of 4,000 people. The first feeding was in Mark; the second of 5,000 in John.

It was another teaching tour for the young Messiah, with sell-out crowds at every stop. Christ may have deliberately taught too long, in the lunch hour, knowing that people would be hungry, especially kids who would need a happy meal from McDonald's by then. Crowd estimates were based on the number of men, so the crowd was possibly larger, including women and children, which made the miracle even more extraordinary!

There they are in the wilderness, which we would call a desert. In other words, there was no 7-Eleven in the neighborhood. The disciples are panicking and may have said, "These people will get crabby if we don't feed them, but how will we do that, Master?" Their Master already knew the answer to the question and the solution to the problem.

With the 4,000 folks, Christ has seven loaves and a few fishes. With the 5.000 folks, He has five loaves and two fishes. It was no coincidence that Christ, the Bread of Life, could and would make mounds of food out of a wee little lunch that wouldn't have been enough for two of His disciples! And there were even left-overs, seven baskets full from the 4000 and 12 baskets from the 5000; funny thing, there was more leftover food after the larger feeding! These *holding patterns* weren't very long; they were quick and concentrated. The disciples only had to wait a short time, but the moments were tense and anxiety-producing. They were worried about the crowd doing a mutiny number on them and Christ's reputation being jeopardized.

Narrative: We've all been there. We panic and go into anxiety mode, and then it's over, like the rear-end accident we avoided. Ever notice how we feel just as exhausted as if it had lasted a week? That's how long we sometimes need to recover, right? Then, later on, we think, well, that wasn't so bad until we hit the next emergency. We have spiritual amnesia. God comes to our rescue in various ways. You were in an accident, but no one was hurt; you were short on your rent, but your landlord extended grace to pay it later. We remember to thank God for deliverance, but we totally forget how God bailed us out the last time when the next crisis comes along! I can almost see the Lord rolling His eyes and saying, "Really?"

Principle: We tend to forget how God got us out of the last holding pattern when we get into the next one!
Perspective: Psalm 78:41-42 "Again and again they turned away and tempted God to kill them, and limited the Holy One of Israel from giving them His blessings. They forgot His power and love and how He had rescued them from their enemies."
Participation: Was there a time when God did a miracle for you in your holding pattern, but you forgot and went into panic mode when the next one came along?

A Blind Man (Mark 10:46-49)

Background: This next event in Christ's ministry occurred in Jericho, only 17 miles northeast of Jerusalem. It was a city adorned with palm trees and balsam gardens which Anthony gave Cleopatra as a gift. Unfortunately, a man named Bartimaeus could not behold the city's immense beauty because he was blind. We don't know how long he was sightless, if he was born that way or if he became that way as a result of a disease or an accident. In John 9, the man was born blind. Either way, in both narratives, we see that these men were blind so that God could manifest His power thru signs and wonders validating His Son as the Light of the World.

Scholars confirm that Timaeus was a man of wealth; his family was well-known by the community as a man of influence. So, his son's situation was likely a source of embarrassment because they could not solve the problem with medical treatment.

It was equally embarrassing to have your blind son begging on the streets for healing. His family undoubtedly tried to restrain him because of the discomfort it brought to them. They considered the request beneath Christ to bother with; an inconvenience of dealing with a minor miracle, as if any miracle was minor! Yet, it wasn't the first or last time Christ went against the prevailing popular opinion. He didn't agree with either of their assumptions. So He wasn't embarrassed by the requestor or considered his begging an interruption, but rather a fulfillment of His ministry.

He didn't agree with the public poll either. (How many think the blind guy should be silent and go home?) Nevertheless, he wouldn't be quiet when told to and called out to Jesus; he even called Him the Son of David. He knew who he was talking to; why else would he risk making a fool of himself? Scholars believe he was persistent because he might have missed Christ coming into Jericho; so he connected with Him on the way out of town; it was his last chance.

Jesus calls him; he gets up, takes off his outer coat, and comes to Jesus as fast as he can, no doubt led by a seeing person so as to not miss this golden opportunity. Then Jesus asks a question to which He already knew the answer. “What do you want me to do for you?” Bartimaeus acknowledges Him as Lord, the personal name for God. God in the flesh tells him to go his way since his faith has made him whole! WOW, what a moment! People could not believe what they saw; a blind man had his sight restored. This was one of six incidents in the ministry of Christ where He healed the blind, so it wasn’t an isolated incident. The Son of God had the power to heal men. The man with sight even signed up to become a follower of The Way, as people who followed Christ were known.

Narrative: Although many of us can see physically, we are often unable to see our way out of our own tunnels, overcome by darkness, and losing direction. Those many long nights of weeping, those never-ending days of discouragement and hopelessness, and the very real malady of depression are all times of darkness when we can’t find our way.

Ever look at a blind person approaching you on the street accompanied by a service dog or walking with a cane? These dear people cannot make it through life without help; they have no choice but to depend on others. When we are in a holding pattern, especially for a longer time, it feels like we are in the dark even though the sun is out. But, unlike the person without the ability to see, we don’t think we need someone to guide us through the danger zone because spiritual blindness isn’t that obvious.

One of the best things we can do in this situation is let someone help us find our way. Maybe one of the reasons for the holding pattern we're in is to make us more dependent upon God and others.

Principle: We need others to guide us through our *holding patterns.*

Perspective: Galatians 6:2 "Share each other's troubles and problems, and so obey our Lord's command."

Participation: What was the darkest point in your life when you felt utterly alone? Who besides the Lord helped you return to the light?

The Centurion and the Servant (Matthew 8:5-13)

Background: For starters, a centurion is a member of a group of 100 Samaritan soldiers who the Roman government paid to keep the Jews in line. So this would not be the most likely guy to believe in a Jewish God or a Messiah, no less! But apparently, he did. This man could put his spiritual indifference and political allegiances aside when facing a crisis. His servant was sick and severely tormented with palsy, a paralysis contracting the joints and causing intense pain, especially in a hotter climate. He had sent the elders first to check Jesus out. And they were almost giddy reporting how great He was and how impressed they were with what He did. But get this: his faith was so great he told Jesus he didn't have to come to the house to do the healing; He could do it long-distance, the next best thing to being there. This guy is in the military reserve; he knows that those under him are told what to do; he simply confirmed his faith in Christ. So, just like the woman at the well, he believed and got rave reviews from Christ for having a faith unlike any He had seen up to this point. (And from a non-Jew!) Can you imagine the headlines on the front page of the Jericho Journal, "Samaritan soldier believes in Jesus!" Most likely, if it was noted at all, it was a teeny article at the end of the recipe section! This centurion first believed in Jesus because of what He could do.

The Jewish leadership didn't mind because they thought the Samaritans were idiots anyway. The article probably said something like, "The guy with the palsy got the meds by the time the centurion got back the next day." But isn't it interesting that the servant was healed at the exact same hour that the centurion asked Jesus to heal him? Purely coincidence. (Uh-huh!) Like other miracles that Jesus did, it was way more important than relieving some guy's joint pain; it was about giving eye-witness evidence of Christ's supernatural person and power. The palsy was a means to a greater end. It was a prophetic forecast of Christ's mission to heal a world paralyzed by sin and the suffering of the pain of self-caused consequences. And by the way, if a half-breed pagan Roman soldier could believe it, how was it that God's own people couldn't or wouldn't? (There's a story there.)

Life's *holding patterns* often involve people who are sick and those who care for them. The soldier and his servant both suffered. The centurion's servant had been ill for a long time, and his boss had been his caretaker.

Narrative: When we have a friend in the hospital, we bring flowers to the patient, visit with them, and pray for them, sometimes forgetting that the family of the one who is ill is struggling for other reasons that are not as obvious. They are in a holding pattern of a different kind but suffering nonetheless.

Principle: A holding pattern is difficult for the ill person but also for those attending them; both struggle differently.

Perspective: John 11:20-21 "When Martha got word that Jesus was coming, she went to meet Him, but Mary stayed at home. Martha said to Jesus, Sir, if you had been here, my brother wouldn't have died."
Participation: Most of us have either been relatives or friends of a patient. They are ill, but we both suffer. Have you been there, yourself? Describe this situation in your life.

Three Siblings (John 11:1-46)
Background: You've probably heard of the singing trio, Peter, Paul, and Mary. Well, try Mary, Martha, and Lazarus. They were close friends of Jesus and spent a lot of time together as He often stayed with them in Bethany, a first-century Airbnb. This was His home away from home in Nazareth, less than one mile from Jerusalem, conveniently located within walking distance so that a lot of people would be there for one of Christ's biggest miracles.

Of course, Christ didn't get there when Lazarus was still alive; that would have made it much less impacting. It would be easier to heal someone who was still alive, right? The disciples kept trying to get Him to move on, stop dilly-dallying around for fear He would wind up late, and His friend would die. They thought they would save Him the embarrassment of not being able to bring a dead man back to life. (Bad press and more fodder for the Pharisee rumor mill!)

They also knew He had become a real threat to the Jewish high officials, and they could take Him out in a public place. But of course, Christ knew the outcome before the planned delay!

On the fourth day, Christ finally shows up. The sisters are trying to be respectful and conceal their irritation. A friend in need is a friend indeed, and the family counted on their friend in high places to come to their brother's rescue. Coming late was also significant because it put Lazarus in an irretrievable state.

According to a first-century Jewish tradition, the fourth day was when the deceased took flight; they went to heaven or hell. But what Christ had done for the widow's son and Jairus's daughter was about to be repeated in this miracle; death would once again be defied.

This was a rehearsal for the final production for Jesus, who would be resurrected from death. Lazarus heard the call and got up in his grave clothes, confirming that he had been dead.

Narrative: Life is like a cross-country road trip, and we get to our destination earlier than we thought. So when our holding pattern is not as long as we thought it would be, we're grateful; it makes up for all the others that turned out to be longer than expected.

Principle: Sometimes, when we expect a more extended holding pattern, it turns out to be shorter, which surprises us and makes us thankful and relieved.
Perspective: John 11:23-24,43 "Jesus told her, Your brother will come back to life again." "Yes, Martha said when everyone else does on Resurrection day." Then He shouted, "Lazarus, come out!"
Participation: What was the shortest holding pattern you have experienced? What emotions accompanied it?

The Prodigal Son (Luke 15)

Background: The theme of this chapter could have been the idea behind the TV show LOST. Christ underscored the reason for His coming into the world to help lost people become found. He used metaphors; a lost sheep, a lost coin, and a lost son to convey this central truth in the parable, as He was en route to Jerusalem to keep His last Passover. It also conveys His intense desire for all who are lost to be found.

Historians concur that although the narrative is parabolic, an earthly story with a heavenly meaning, it is more likely based on a real-life family situation with which Jesus was familiar. The family was one of wealth. Theirs was a culture where inheritances were often given to the benefactors before the death of a parent. Also, it was not uncommon for affluent families to send their children to prestigious places like Carthage, Alexandria, Antioch, or Rome for education or cultural exposure.

However, in this case, the renegade son had no intention of furthering his education; he was headed to the big city to party hearty. Ironically, the details of the hedonistic escapade, like the BC version of Hugh Hefner, might have been omitted from the narrative, giving the older brother less evidence for incriminating his younger brother.

You know the storyline; the younger brother is now broke, working as second in command in a pigpen. (By the way, what could be more offensive to a Jew?) This all adds insult to injury. To boot, he would eat a diet of bean-shaped pods from the carob tree often used for food by the poor.

Yet, the real significance is not why and how he left but why he came home. Crisis often brings us closer. No money and pig food did him in. He pondered how foolish he had been, what life would be like at home, and in desperation, decided to return. He would go home to his father, convinced he would be disowned. (Good luck getting your inheritance twice!)

The earthly father is a picture of our heavenly Father, one waiting and looking for the son to return, embracing him with tears, giving him a festal welcome back. But on the other hand, the earthly brother is a picture of religious leaders who considered themselves superior to sinners they refused to forgive and receive. Thus, it tells us that the older brother referred to his delinquent brother as *your* son when addressing his father, implying that he had disowned him and denied him as his brother.

All three men in this parable were in *holding patterns.* (Do the math). The younger son was away from home for an extended time. How long did it take for his funds to run out? How long was he in the pigpen? The father was without his son, during which time he was filled with worry, anxiety, and perhaps guilt, wondering if he would ever see him again. The older son was probably pondering what would happen if the party boy ran out of money. Could I get his share of the inheritance if he doesn't show up?

This three-pronged holding pattern is unique from any we have explored so far. Three different people are in the same holding pattern, which began when the young son left and ended when he returned. None of them knew how long it would be, although the longer it went, the more they were convinced that it would never end. Two of them hoped it would; one of them didn't.

Narrative: We may prefer the status quo and the pain of staying the same rather than the pain of becoming different. We don't want to change. Professional students, addicts, or chronic complainers really like *holding patterns* rather than ending them.

To change or not to change, that is the question. We don't or won't change because we fear it will hurt and cause us pain. Even if it's good for us, we don't take the risk because we fear the unknown. Or we may wonder if we can sustain the change. But if we get tired of the same, we need to break with the past and discover that being willing to change has its benefits. We feel better about ourselves, feel released from acting, and have greater confidence about life in general. So we have to decide: Do we want to endure the greater pain of staying sick or the lesser pain of getting well?

Principle: Breaking out of a holding pattern may require risk and pain. However, staying the same may be more painful than changing.
Perspective: Psalm 32:4-5 "All day and all night your hand was heavy on me. My strength evaporated like water on a sunny day until I finally admitted all my sins to you and stopped trying to hide them. I said to myself, I will confess them to the Lord. And you forgave me! All my guilt is gone."
Participation: Have you ever been in a self-caused holding pattern that required risking pain to change? Did you change or stay the same? What happened?

A Family (Mark 3:31-33)
Background: This was no run-of-the-mill family; it was Christ's family, His earthly mother, His stepbrothers, and stepsisters. It may also have included His cousins, two of

whom Jesus had already chosen to be His disciples. The text doesn't mention Jesus' earthly father. Here's the scenario: Jesus was on a teaching tour, perhaps a biblical equivalent to Dr. Phil on a lecture circuit. He is also undoubtedly neck-deep in thoughtful theological discourse when interrupted by His tour manager, who informs Him that His relatives have arrived and want to see Him. For starters, there must have been standing room only for His star appearance; His mother and others didn't have reserved seats; they saunter up and say howdy. So they pass a note to the host, who feels compelled to hand it to Jesus. (It would be like the First Family being made to sit in the bleachers while the President is giving the State of the Union address.)

The other exciting tidbit was why they needed to see Him at that very moment. (Wouldn't they see Him at home for dinner or before He left for work in the morning?) There was a divine reason for the interruption. The religious leaders were hot on Christ's trial, breathing down His neck after the healing of a man's withered hand. (Wouldn't you know He had done it again, maybe on purpose?)

So Mary, being the concerned, caring mother with maternal intuition, wants to protect her son, taking Him out of harm's way. And no doubt with the family nodding amens in the background asking, "Does He know what He is doing?" That's just it. He knew exactly what He was doing and why He was doing it. So what does Jesus do? Does He publicly put them down for interrupting His speech and mission to change the world forever? Does He excuse Himself politely and speak with them, thanking them for their concern and telling them He will explain things later? Does He avoid the issue altogether or use it as a teaching moment?

Rather than excuse His confused but caring clan, He breaks from His PowerPoint presentation and asks a question. Who are my actual relatives? They are those who do the will of my Father, believe in me, and are made a part of God's family.

It probably embarrassed those folks in the back row. But we must give Mary and the other siblings kudos for trying to watch out for Jesus. After all, Christ was a handful! But, we also have to put ourselves in His family's sandals. They didn't know how long Jesus had left on earth; they didn't want Him to mess up and get killed. He was only thirty and had His whole life before Him. He was a nice guy, and they wanted Him around as long as possible if He would stay away from those perturbing Pharisees!

Mary knew about all those things. She undoubtedly knew what was ahead for Him but still wanted His life to be somewhat normal. She would live to see what He would turn out to be and what would happen to Him. As the Heavenly Parent, God knew what it was to enter a holding pattern and wait for it to end; the agonizing death of His son was exactly what He had designed for Him and for the world. But for God and Mary, it didn't make the holding pattern any easier. Nonetheless, from a human standpoint, His earthly family tried to get Him to do *their* plan for His life rather than God's! (Sound familiar?)

Narrative: Don't you just love those folks who must work for the FBI the way they seem to know everything usually from the neighborhood hotline or office grapevine? They never mind their own business because they have their nose in everybody else's, all under the guise of caring for others, of course. But, some people need to get a life by not interfering with yours. It's unlikely that anyone else will go through their holding pattern exactly as you go through yours!

Principle: One thing that makes *holding patterns* difficult is when well-meaning people try to second guess what we are doing and why we are doing it!
Perspective: Micah 7:6b "A man's enemies will be found in his own home."
Participation: Most of us have experienced conflict with family members or well-meaning friends who make life challenging. What has been your experience? How has it affected you?

The Disciples (Luke 9:1-9)
Background: The team is only as good as their coach. Had we been alive in Christ's day and asked Him about the team, it probably got mixed reviews. He had chosen each one by careful prayer to His Father, who granted Him the discernment needed to choose them. Yet, He knew they were mere human beings with a young, fragile faith that would be ruthlessly tested by the demands of ministry and the hostile reaction to the gospel, bringing about persecution and death. Thus, it was understandable that He would have reservations sending them out on the first of many missions.

They were called and commissioned to preach the kingdom of God by His power and authority over devils and disease. By casting out demons and curing sickness, they would validate the truth of their message, not a minor assignment for a bunch of rookies with little experience outside of catching fish and collecting taxes.

In this tentative situation, the single redemptive element was that these twelve men would share something in common; they were ordinary men given extraordinary power. Their God had not called them for something He could not equip them to do. The only possible explanation for what they did was that they didn't do it themselves! This reality was underscored by the strange instructions He gave them for their inaugural mission. They were to travel lightly, with no walking sticks, script, money, food, and only one outer coat and one pair of sandals. They would not have had any motel reservations; they would bunk with whoever liked them and invited them in. This would be easier in their eastern culture, where it was customary to offer hospitality to strangers who would then have complete protection inside their walls.

There were often unique houses in neighborhoods designated as hotel-like accommodations to welcome and protect travelers. These homes often furthered the mission work, as notated in the Book of Acts. Christ forecasted that not everyone would get a key to the city for having His motley crew of disciples in their town or at their door. At least they went out by two; it was easier and safer not to travel alone, especially in those times. If and when refused, they were to leave the city and shake the dust off their sandals, a custom the Jews practiced when returning to the Holy Land from Gentile nations.

Ironically, these were the very nations to which the Gospel of the Kingdom would be extended through their mission. The disciples did not want to ask Christ how long they would be on their mission. They didn't want to seem uncooperative or disloyal. The answer to the question? The rest of their lives!

The disciples knew they had been chosen and commissioned by the God of Abraham, Isaac, and Jacob to take the most important message globally, with the results extending into eternity. They also knew that they were mere humans who had the same emotions anyone else would have had! They had a strong suspicion that their leader would leave them after a short time, and they would have to face the astronomical assignment on their own, and their message would be branded as heretical and their lives endangered. No recruiter would be successful in signing up new members given these requirements.

Narrative: The boss calls you in and lets you know he has volunteered you to head a project in the aerodynamics department; way outside your wheelhouse, and your stomach goes into a knot the size of Alaska. You don't feel honored but overwhelmed, knowing that your future with the company and your pay raise are attached to accepting the assignment. Suddenly you know how you will spend the next year of your once-happy life. You know how long your holding pattern will be and wish you didn't!

Principle: *Holding patterns* can often require doing something above our pay grade, yet we have no choice.
Perspective: Luke 1:30-31 "Don't be frightened, Mary, the angel told her, for God has decided to wonderfully bless you! You will soon become pregnant and have a baby boy, and you are to name Him Jesus."
Participation: Have you ever had an assignment that seemed way too hard to do? What did you do when you found yourself in this predicament? What good came to you, if any, from this experience?

The Transfiguration (Matthew 17:1-11)
Background: It is no surprise that Matthew included the transfiguration in his gospel. The reason? It confirms Christ as the Messiah, a fundamental fact to the Jews, the central audience of the writer. Mark writes primarily to the Gentiles, Luke to the Greeks, and John to everyone else.

This encounter was between Christ and His inner circle of disciples, Peter, James, and John; it was purportedly at night. (When the celestial fireworks could be more visible!) It took place at the end of six days, thus on the seventh day, corresponding with the seventh day of creation and the Old Testament Sabbath. Finally, it took place on an unnamed mountain. Anonymity was necessary at this point in Christ's mission.

This spontaneous epiphany was for Christ to assure His followers He was who He claimed to be, God in human form sent by His Heavenly Father. He was more than simply conceptual; He was visible, based on eye-witness, an in-your-face reality. It had all these components. However, it is interesting that the three men were told not to tell anyone about it. The publicity was pre-mature and potentially dangerous.

Christ was literally transformed/transfigured before them. They could see but not believe their eyes! They saw Christ turned inside out, all of His inner glory as God revealed outwardly through Him as a man. This was the New Testament version of the Shekinah Glory that led Israel through the wilderness and appeared to Moses on Mt. Sinai at the giving of the Law. Remember that no one was allowed to see God in the Old Testament at any time. The transfiguration of Christ was one of the first times anyone had seen God. The first time was when God opened the heavens and affirmed Him as His beloved Son when baptized by John the Baptist.

But that's not all; guess who else showed up? Moses and Elijah. Yep, the two guys who were caught up into heaven! (Like an Old Testament rapture.) The glory of God blinded the trio of dazzled disciples. But the topic of discussion was different than what you might have expected.

The subject of the world's salvation was essential to Moses and Elijah because they got to see the fulfillment of the Messianic prophecy, the Savior who had finally come to rescue His people. Moses had rescued his people from Egypt; Elijah had rescued them from their enemies. Moses represented the Law, and Elijah represented the Prophets. But, of course, their showing up was only a forecast or a foreshadowing of what was to come; they wanted and got to realize their hope.

But even a front-row seat in heaven would have been no match for the one they had on earth! Seeing Christ transformed was one thing; having Old Testament rock stars was more than the disciples could take. And what's more interesting, Moses and Elijah will show up again on earth during the Great Tribulation to deliver a message about Christ. His second appearance will be to judge the world for rejecting Him the first time!

The transfiguration reveals a holding pattern somewhat different than the others in two aspects. First, it was short, one evening, but intensive. It wasn't emotionally painful like that of Abraham and Isaac or physically painful as for the three men in the fiery furnace. On the contrary, it was exciting and pleasurable. (An invitation to the premiere of Christ as you've never seen Him). Secondly, the honored guests didn't want it to end, literally. We know that in part because Peter, impulsive as usual, wanted to build neat and tidy tabernacles to house the royal visitors. But no one was to stay longer. Christ, Moses and Elijah weren't to live in earthly buildings made with hands.

Narrative: Who wouldn't want an around-the-world cruise to be extended or an evening with classmates at your 50th class reunion? But because of sin, life could not be a perpetual permanent party!

God allowed our first parents to choose which life they wanted. They had the perfect, hassle-free life but traded it for a perverted, fallen one where they lived out the consequences of their choices, a life we inherited.

Principle: We can't make pleasurable *holding patterns* last indefinitely. They wouldn't mean as much; we wouldn't grow as much.

Perspective: Ecclesiastes 5:19-20 "It is very good if a man has received wealth from the Lord and the good health to enjoy it. To enjoy your work and accept your lot in life is indeed a gift from God. The person who does that will not need to look back with sorrow on his past, for God gives him joy."

Participation: Select one of your favorite *holding patterns*. Why did you want it to last?

Christ's Culmination of Ministry
The Betrayal (John 13:1-30)

Background: The betrayal of Christ is one of the few events in the life of Christ to be recorded by all four gospel writers. John's account was the most enduring due to his intimate relationship with the Lord. Christ's time had come, not a minute sooner than it was supposed to, not with the Pharisees closing in on Him like a caged animal; not until His Father said, time is up, this is it. And although Christ had known about this hour before time and gave up the splendors of heaven for the muck of earth, He no doubt had mixed emotions about it; the time had finally come, but He wished it hadn't.

Nevertheless, Judas knew what he had to do, which wasn't pretty. But what would make it uglier was that one of Christ's own would be the means of His being apprehended, brought to trial, and put to death. The betrayer was one of the twelve He had poured His life into for three years, knew Him, heard Him teach, seen Him do miracles, one who had claimed to be a

Christ-follower. What true disciple of Christ would think the way Judas did or do what he was about to do?

But he figured if Christ was hauled into court and even put to death, He could handle the opposition. In fact, Christ could have stopped the betrayal or the crucifixion. Judas didn't understand two things about predictions. One, Christ was to be handed over to sinful men, religious leaders, and soldiers. He didn't need to be betrayed to be identified. Two, He wasn't supposed to overcome the opposition...yet!

But Judas will always be remembered as the mole, the guy who didn't have Christ's back, the one who instead stabbed Him in the back. Yet what is so significant about the betrayal is that Christ wasn't focused on Himself but on those He was about to save. He knew He had a divine destiny, to redeem humankind from the hold of the Devil and his hold on humanity; He was about to turn the course of human history around and overturn His unholy opponent. This was evident in the last supper He shared with His still bewildered followers. It was the Passover Supper in which Christ took the old elements of bread and wine, made the New Testament elements of His broken body, and shed blood, the Lord's Supper.

This was a memorial meal hosted by the Living Pascal Lamb. Unlike the animal used as temporal sacrifices, He would be a permanent offering. The Lamb of God would do what the Law would never do, bring the world to God. Yet, on this night, the eternal Savior became the ultimate servant.

He proved this by washing the feet of His motley crew, one which repulsed Peter, who said, 'Oh no, Lord; you're not washing my feet.' But upon understanding what it meant, he said, 'Lord, give me a bath!' Christ then served them a meal they and the world would never forget, their communion with

Him memorialized forever. In His darkest hour, He focused on the needs of others instead of His own. He would lay down His life rather than set up His kingdom.

Judas, the betrayer, did not stay for the whole celebration; he was off to do his dirty deed, driven by the devil who had stolen his heart and taken control of his senses. The devil didn't make Judas do it; he chose to follow and obey the evil one. He was on a malicious mission for which he ended his life. He was indirectly responsible for the death of his friend, killing the very Son of God. Although the betrayal was predicted, Judas was still held responsible for being a traitor. He became a first-century Benedict Arnold.

Paul and Judas were complete opposites. They had nothing in common except being on the same team for a short season. One remained, and the other defected. Both experienced *holding patterns*. Christ waited for some three and a half years for what He knew was inevitable, His betrayal at the hand of one of His disciples, desertion by the rest, the humiliating trial, the incredulous suffering, and His ignominious death. He knew everything that would happen and when it would happen.

Narrative: Sometimes, we wonder why God doesn't tell us what will happen before it does. Wouldn't it just be easier if we knew what, when, and how things would play out? Really? How much faith would it take if we knew everything in advance, and why would we need to pray? Instead, we would be caught in a web of worry about what was coming and if we could handle it until it was over. We often don't know how long the holding pattern will last. But, we do know *who* it is who will get us through. (Job's Old Testament lesson).

We must wonder why God allows these things to happen, but blaming Him or anybody else does not solve the problem. We have to face our issues and often get the help of others, like pastors, counselors, or trusted friends. These resources can help us work through our guilt, our need to forgive, and our need for revenge. But the one who can help us most is the One who allowed things to happen and gives us the resources by which to deal with them. He knows but does not force the outcome; He is a true gentleman. He allows us the freedom to choose our reactions.

Principle: Our *holding patterns* require faith in the One who allows them and helps us deal with the outcome.
Perspective: Hebrews 11:8 "Abraham trusted God, and when God told him to leave home and go far away to another land that He promised to give him, Abraham obeyed. Away he went, not even knowing where he was going."
Participation: Reflect on a time when you could not handle something significant in your life but simply had to trust God to help you deal with it.

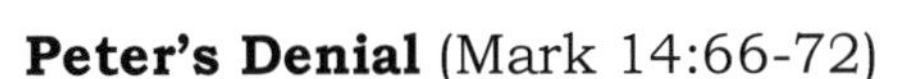

Peter's Denial (Mark 14:66-72)
Background: Finding the shortest Gospel's most extended and detailed narrative is engaging. Peter's nickname, the rock, was appropriately given to the man whose action impacted all those around him. The passionate side of Peter was motivational, i.e., he got out of the boat and walked on water to get to Jesus. But the impulsive side of Peter could be harmful. He told Jesus He wasn't supposed to suffer and that he'd never betray Him. Yet the night before Christ's death became one of the darkest moments for Peter and the Lord he professed to believe in, love, and follow. The description of the incident is a composite of three Gospels. Nevertheless, it appears to have a commonality. Peter pretended to be simply an on-looker who, when asked about his identity, claimed he did not know who Christ was.

Suspicious bystanders challenged Peter about his association with the recently accused; a good man now branded a criminal. (A clue to Peter's responses!) These unknown nobodies simply sought information but had no power to get him in trouble for knowing and hanging out with Jesus. There were three denials just as Christ had predicted: One, to Caiaphas's doorkeeper. Two, a denial with an oath made. Three, he cursed and swore he did not know Jesus. (Like putting your hand on a Bible swearing to tell the whole truth, so help you, God) His denial increased with intensity after each inquisition.

The first problem with this denial was Peter's promise never to deny his Savior. 'I will always be true to you and never leave you, my Lord.' Within minutes of Christ being apprehended in the garden and taken to trial, Peter had reneged on all that. He no doubt wrestled with the same issues the other disciples did. Christ wasn't supposed to suffer but instead make Israel's enemies suffer, not to look bad in front of his Jewish and non-Jewish opponents but to show them up. Peter and the gang hadn't planned on teaming up with a loser.

But it was Peter's luck to be hanging out close enough to the action and be in the wrong place at the wrong time and get recognized. The fire around which he stood and warmed himself on the still cold April night in AD 33 probably clearly silhouetted his unmistakable Jewish features. After all, he was one of the big three disciples; a lot of people had seen him with his Master. (Not to mention the Galilean accent.) But "No," he contended passionately, of course. "I don't know who you're talking about."

The word denial in the original language of the New Testament means to disown, deny, or simply not believe that something even existed. And there was another critical element in this episode. The rooster crowing to indicate what Peter had done confirms Christ's knowing ahead of time and picking Peter to be His disciple anyway, the *second* one to betray him! So Judas and Peter were co-traitors!

Peter clearly focused on self-protection and forgot that his Savior was embroiled in an illegal trial at night so that people wouldn't know about it. Therefore, Christ needed as much support as He could, especially with the imminent betrayals. Even the high priest, Caiaphas, acknowledged who Christ was!

The second crowing was at five or six o'clock in the morning, giving us some idea of how long the trial took. Between the first and second crowing is when Peter denied his Lord. He had plenty of time to realize what he was doing. It wasn't simply a slip of the tongue. The two sadder elements of this story were yet to come. First, as Christ was led through the court of Caiaphas, He no doubt looked at Peter with a look that words could not have described. Second, Christ has been betrayed by His own, by those He trusted to follow Him anywhere and be loyal to Him. Peter, the one upon whose faith Christ would build His church, deserted Him on the worst night of His life in the hour of His greatest need.

Secondly, when Peter knew he had fulfilled the promised prediction, he wept bitterly, as only recorded by Matthew and Mark. The original word for weep means he was literally doubled over; his was a long and continual sob fest. How else could he feel but terrible about who he was and what he had done? Peter was guilty of endangering the one he professed to trust, the one who had so trusted him. Now, he wondered, was he worthless, of no value to Christ, unforgivable and unpardonable? How would he make it up to his Master, the one he professed to love but hurt so terribly?

Narrative: We only hurt the ones we love. Anyone wounded by a family member or dear friend knows how this feels. This is because the greatest hurt involves the people we're closest to. There are reasons for that. We feel rejected and devaluated. A family is to be most loyal to their own. Rejection hurts deeply and takes longer to heal.

Principle: *Holding patterns* often involve being hurt by those we love and then having to endure the pain of an unresolved relationship.

Perspective: Psalm 55:12-14 "It was not an enemy who taunted me, then I could have borne it; I could have hidden and escaped. But it was you, a man like myself, my companion and my friend. What fellowship we had, what wonderful discussions as we walked together to the Temple of the Lord on holy days."

Participation: Have you ever betrayed or turned on someone you loved and were close to? Did someone treat you in the same way? What would you do differently if you got a chance to change your history?

The Crucifixion *of Christ* (Mark 15)

Background: It may strike you as odd that we would take the narrative of Christ's crucifixion from the shortest of the Gospels, one based on data more than a personal account format. Yet, Mark states it succinctly with a minimum of sentiment. His Gospel became the basis of the other three Gospels; he gave us the bones; the other apostles put the meat on them. Remember, Mark wrote primarily to the Gentile audience. He emphasized how non-Jews responded to Jesus, their Savior, who came to save both Jew and Gentile. The Roman world showed little respect or tolerance for a group of religious zealots who spoke a different language and worshiped God instead of their smorgasbord of gods. They, like Judas, did not know that they were fulfilling prophecies as far back as Moses, David, and the Old Testament prophets in exact detail. They would put Christ to death; they would kill God.

They played into the hands of the one whose hands they pierced with spikes. They would inflict the cruelest form of punishment known to man, which was banned by later civilizations. It was a punishment deserved by criminals, not an innocent man who went around doing good, helping everyone, hurting no one. Thus the emotional pain was commensurate with the physical pain Christ endured, one He refused to numb with a narcotic but was shortened by His merciful Father. God had seen His Son suffer enough.

The very people who heard His messages and saw His miracles turned on Him. Even His disciples still doubted the credibility of His person and work, especially since He had not proven to have the power to free them from their enemies. They were torn between being loyal but keenly disappointed. The dual reality of the crucifixion was that it was both avoidable yet inevitable.

At any moment, Christ could have summoned countless angelic forces of the heavens to rescue Him and renounce His captors and killers. He could have dismounted the cross and had a different final word: "Father, forgive them for they know not what they do." It could have been, 'Father, get them and give them what they've got coming.' But He didn't do that. If only He had, He would have overcome the worldly power and set up only a temporary earthly kingdom for a season. Instead, He overcame the Evil One who had taken control of the world. Christ set up a kingdom that would never end. It was the easiest yet hardest, simplest but most difficult, choice for Him to make. Christ suffered in flesh and spirit more than any other human being in all of history. Many others have suffered but not paid the price of redeeming us from sin, going to the grave, and conquering death. Jesus Christ made death to die.

The testimony of the puppet ruler, Pilate, placed in power by the Romans, gave credentials to Christ, the true King of the Jews. Pilate had this title inscribed above Christ's bleeding head in three known languages; Hebrew, Greek, and Aramaic. Yet this death was no mistake; it was enacted by divine purpose to fulfill God's ultimate plan for the world. Thus, good Friday was good because the Sunday that followed undid the work of the Devil. Christ defied death and brought light into darkness.

Can we begin to fathom or attempt to identify with Christ's holding pattern of horrific pain in every aspect of His life, physically, emotionally, and relationally? The length of the holding pattern would have seemed interminable. That's how you and I would have felt. We deserved it like the two convicts who book-ended Him on the cross. He didn't. Thus, it was the holding pattern above all others. But yet He chose to focus on us, not Himself. Amazing Grace!

Narrative: One of the greatest things about being on hold is that we get to help others in some way. Unless you want to host a pity party for yourself and invite all your cronies to commiserate with you, focusing on the needs of others is not only the right idea; it gets our minds off ourselves. Just because our life is on hold doesn't mean we can't invest time and energy in someone else's life.

Principle: A holding pattern can sometimes allow us to focus on the needs of others more than our own.

Perspective: Hebrews 2:17 "And it was necessary for Jesus to be like us, His brothers, so that He could be our merciful and faithful High Priest before God, a Priest who would be both

merciful to us and faithful to God in dealing with the sins of the people."
Participation: Write out three reasons why focusing on others in any situation is profitable.

The Disciples (John 20:19-31)
Background: Christ knew He had disciple problems when they weren't all there with confetti and a 'welcome back Jesus' sign at the tomb. He found them, of course; He knew right where they were and simply went through the wall to get into the room where they were hiding. It was a lock-in, alright, but one full of fear, not fun. It was one of two appearances, one on Resurrection Sunday itself and again eight days later, one of many times in the next forty days. The same scenario was recorded in Mark and Luke with a few variations. In Mark, Jesus scolded them for not believing; in Luke, He ate with them to confirm that He was a real live person. In John's account, He let Thomas, the doubter, touch His hands and His side, who said he would not believe until he did. Then Christ gave other signs in their midst proving that He was alive and the resurrected Lord He had forecasted to be. But were they revved up enough to begin their co-mission? Not quite!

They were in hiding because their leader had been taken from them. They had seen Him the last time before they ran from Him in Gethsemane; some had last seen Him dying or dead on the cross. Their leader, the last hope of Israel, had failed them; He had let His nation down. It was still under the rule of the Romans. Moreover, they knew that if Christ were still dead, the Romans would soon kill them! They were conflicted. But here was Christ fully recovered from the savage beating and crucifixion, talking with them, showing them His injured body. He ate with them and commanded them to go and change the world thru His message, one He had just validated! They were still trying to get their minds around what had just happened and what it meant for the future after leaving the room. They were between the proverbial rock and a hard place.

Narrative: Sometimes, people don't know how to get through their *holding patterns*. They are trapped between the past and the future. They're afraid to venture forth, certain they could never find the right person or job. So they cut themselves off from everyone and choose to suffer in solitude. They wait alone and resign themselves to a hopeless future. So it is essential to maintain as regular a routine as possible during our *holding patterns*; keeping active, taking your mind off yourself, and focusing on future possibilities.

Principle: The guilt of the past and fear of the future often cause us to be immobilized in the present. We become immobilized rather than energized because we do not have hope!

Perspective: Exodus 14:13-14 "But Moses told the people, don't be afraid. Just stand where you are and watch, and you will see the wonderful way the Lord will rescue you today. The Egyptians you remember, you will never see them again. The Lord will fight for you, and you won't need to lift a finger!"

Participation: Have you ever been stuck in the present? What did you do to get unstuck and move on? If not, how could your faith help you deal with the past and face the future?

The Resurrection and Ascension (Mark 16 Luke 24)
Background: The empty cross and the empty tomb became the cornerstone of the church built on the rock of faith in the Living Christ against which the gates of hell would not prevail. The followers of Christ knew about the prediction; they would be in a holding pattern before He returned to change everything. He had established Himself as the only religious figure to overcome death. Death was only a comma, not a period in His life and ministry narrative. Mark and Luke were the only two who recorded it, one in the Gospel and the other in the book of Acts. This was a theophany; literally, God showed up. He became visible to humanity; Christ gave God a face.

After returning from the dead, He entered into a 40-day tour with His disciples; plenty of time for people to see that He had indeed risen, substantiated by eye-witness accounts. So the cowardly disciples were finally convinced. He was now confident in them, giving them the power and authority to complete their divine assignment. It was underscored by the assurance that He would be with them until the end of the age; they had no idea how long that would be!

So, they faced a dilemma. Ending a short holding pattern simply introduced another. Key question; how long would the second holding pattern last? How long before He came back the next time? The Jews living at that time expected it to be in their lifetime; Christ had inferred that this generation would see the coming of Christ the second time. Thus, they had reasons to speculate that the second holding pattern would be the length of a generation, 40 years. In the meantime, He would be present by leaving, which seemed like a contradiction. The world is still waiting for His return.

The whole of life has become one big holding pattern made up of lots of little ones. Usually, getting thru one makes us better able to handle the ones that follow. It worked for the disciples! In this case, the first one was hard, but the next one was easier; coming out of hiding to see Christ for the last time and then depart to heaven.

Narrative: Often, one holding pattern prepares you for the next one! I know; good grief, how many times do we have to go thru this in a lifetime? Only God knows and knows all about *holding patterns* ahead of time. (Some consolation!) Sometimes the *holding patterns* get harder, and sometimes they get easier. Whatever the case, maybe we become stronger with spiritual muscle and greater endurance by going through times of waiting.

Principle: *Holding patterns* are consecutive, each for a different purpose.

Perspective: Genesis 22:11-12 "At that moment, the Angel of God shouted to him from heaven, Abraham! Abraham! Yes, Lord, he answered. Lay down the knife; don't hurt the lad in any way, the Angel said, for I know that God is first in your life, you have not withheld even your beloved son from me."

Participation: Can you track a similar back-to-back experience as the disciples faced? If so, how did the first experience prepare you for the second?

The Last Days and Second Coming of Christ (Matthew 24, Mark 13, Luke 21)

Background: Only three of the gospels recorded the end-time forecast. Whenever a theme appears in more than one gospel, it deserves special attention. This is especially true when the day's sermon had to do with what was happening for the next 2000 years, as forecasted by the Apostle John given it on the island of Patmos. Christ gave this information to His disciples on Monday of Holy Week, the last week of His life on earth. But there would be a giant gap between the forecast and the end-time events, which included: wars, famines, earthquakes, persecution, false prophets, and *significant* changes in the heavens and earth.

There would be false prophets pretending to be Christ. There were 29 such false prophets in Christ's day, followed by those throughout history, culminating in the final false prophet, the anti-Christ. These happenings will demonstrate God's wrath toward a rebellious world that has rejected His greatness, authority, and truth. God promised Noah that He would not destroy the world again by a flood, but He also promised to destroy it by fire. He compared our day to Noah's as both cultures have adopted the mantra, 'Let's eat, drink and be merry, for tomorrow we die.' No more accurate word was ever spoken by two groups of people who would choose to die in their sin rather than choose life through faith in the true Christ. They would believe a lie and face ultimate judgment.

Many scoffers of all ages have dismissed these biblical forecasts. Why? We've always had these things throughout history, so what's the difference? The difference is three-fold; the frequency and intensity of the events and the spirit of anarchy are unequaled in the world's history. The last one is based on the fact that the Evil One knows that his time is getting shorter before the end of the world and the return of Christ. Thus Satan becomes more desperate and ruthless. He knows he has already lost, so all he can do is keep people from knowing and growing in their relationship with God. In simple terms, he does all the damage he can before he is deported to Hell permanently.

The Son of God will appear in great glory and be seen by the entire world at once. Many scholars speculate that He will come in a cross-shaped cloud. All believers in Christ will be gathered together for a heavenly reunion. He will defeat His enemies with a single word. This last great war will become an eternal triumph for the commander and chief of the forces of heaven and earth.

His parousia, His visible presence, will cause both rejoicing and remorse. Rejoicing for those who have entrusted their lives to Him and await heaven with Him and remorse for those who haven't received Him and face eternal separation from Him. The Word of God and the Living Word will outlast the world; heaven and earth will pass away. He will re-make and configure the two into one. It will become the eternal residence of the redeemed, with the New Jerusalem as its capital.

How did the disciples respond to this end-time narrative? The exchange wasn't so much a dialogue as a monologue; Christ did all the talking. There is no record of the disciples reacting, but we can be pretty sure they didn't doze off. His final command was to take heed, endure, pray and watch. There was no hour-long Q and A session except the introductory ones when the disciples asked, "When will these things be, and what will be the sign of your coming at the end of the world?" (Matthew 23:3 NIV)

We, too, can be reasonably confident that most *holding patterns* deal with involve chaos, disorder, a change of life routine, and a disruption of the status quo. The beleaguered band of Christ's followers knew that either way, close or far away in time, their lives and the life of the world would never be the same!

Narrative: Some positive things accompany the forecast; the Gospel will be preached to the ends of the earth using diversified technology. Churches had to go online during the pandemic, yet they began reaching those who never attended in person. But, it's one thing to have faith when times are good but more challenging when they're not. The closer we get to the end of the world, it may mean that our faith and belief system will be significantly tested. The anti-Christian culture will try our faith to see what it's really made of, whether it costs us something or if it's only a matter of convenience.

It has been said that Christians are like teabags; their true strength comes out in hot water! So we could well be wondering how long the holding pattern of all of human history will last; you know, the one between the first creation of the world and the second one when God makes a whole new heaven and earth. Only God knows how long the *holding patterns* will last and when they will end. (Thank God someone knows and controls it all!)

Principle: *Holding patterns* are often a time of disruption and change, creating uncertainty and anxiety over how things will turn out ultimately for us and our world.
Perspective: II Peter 3:11-13 "And so since everything around us is going to melt away, what holy, godly lives we should be living! You should look forward to that day and hurry it along, the day when God will set the heavens on fire, and the heavenly bodies will melt and disappear in flames. But we are looking forward to God's promise of new heavens and a new earth afterwards, where there will be only goodness."
Participation: What current events indicate we may be in the holding pattern of the last days? What should you do to prepare for them?

Historical Books
Acts of the Apostles

The Wait for Christ's Return (Acts1:8)

Background: The opening chapter of Luke's second book culminates with ten appearances of Christ to His followers and over 500 others. The one crucified becomes the one glorified over the weekend. His Resurrection tour lasted 40 days, underscoring His real-life appearance and more miracles than He had done before His death. The title of the Author of Salvation could only be bestowed on Him after His death. (Hebrews 12:1-3) Three *holding patterns* were present. The first required waiting in Jerusalem for the coming of the Holy Spirit, who would baptize His followers differently from John the Baptist. The second was waiting for their commissioning to the ends of the earth. The third was waiting for Him to return after He promised to return in the way He left, in the clouds, confirmed by two angels. The one who had come as a baby and left as a man, the Son of God, had redeemed and would rule the world. Christ commissioned them to carry out the mission, with one big difference, without Him: A significant omission became the basis of the co-mission.

Narrative: The disciples had a significant advantage over everyone who lived before and after them. God was visible to them. They could see Him, hear Him, and be with Him! The rest of us can only read about Him. We can't look up and see Him, talk with Him directly, or feel His hand on our shoulder. We must go through and get through our waiting zones with faith in the invisible, the God out there somewhere. He can seem distant and detached from us. Contrary to our modern pragmatic world where seeing is believing, we operate on a different algorithm; *believing is seeing*!

Principle: While on hold, we simply believe God is invisibly present through our *holding patterns*.

Perspective: Psalm 22:1-2 "My God, my God, why have you forsaken me? Why do you refuse to help me or even to listen to my groans? Day and night, I keep on weeping, crying for your help, but there is no reply."
Participation: Was there ever a holding pattern in your life when you felt God was not really present? How did that make you feel?

The Lame Man (Acts 3:1-6)
Background: This story begins with a holding pattern. A man lame from birth was at the Beautiful Gate, where he was carried daily. (Not unlike the man at the pool in Christ's healing ministry.) But, he got more than money; he got a miracle. This continuation of Christ's ministry emboldened and enabled His disciples to set the context for another sermon by Peter. As part of his message, he gives an altar call. He tells people to repent to change their thinking, acting, and life direction. They not only needed to be redeemed from sin but be refreshed by the presence of the Lord. Christ would bring restitution to all things just as the prophets promised from the beginning of the world. The Ultimate Prophet had come but was yet to come again. They were to wait for His return.

Five hundred people now waited to see if Christ would be a show or no-show. The disciples and the converts had a single hope; that Christ would set up His kingdom immediately. The lame man waited to be healed. The early church also had to wait for Christ's return. The kingdom would come; it was not a matter of **if** but **when**!

Narrative: In our instant gratification culture, we don't want to wait for anything and certainly not get trapped in a holding pattern longer than it takes someone to vacate the parking place we want at Costco! But since that is not an option, we would at least like to design our own holding pattern. Ah, but it doesn't work that way. God, the master designer of life, regulates those times in our lives, whether we like it or not. And they are ultimately for our good, no matter how bad they seem to us at the time. Sometimes it's hard for us to hear that, but God doesn't make mistakes, and He takes His time, but He is never late. God allows everything because He loves me and wants me to be the best person I was made to be. *Holding patterns* are a means to that end, that's right. And believe me, I know how you are feeling right about now!

Principle: God comes thru for us in our *holding patterns* on His terms and on His timetable.
Perspective: John 11:39-40 "Roll the stone aside, Jesus told them. But Martha, the dead man's sister, said, by now, the smell will be terrible, for he has been dead four days. But didn't I tell you that you will see a wonderful miracle from God if you believe?"
Participation: Look back to a happening where the timing seemed bad. Can you see now that the timing worked for good?

Ananias and Sapphira (Acts 5:1-11)
Background: The following holding pattern is one of the most frightening in the scriptures. It involves two active church members, well known in the Christian community, which made their deadly mistake so tragic. Ananias and Sapphira. Her name was based on the sapphire stone, which meant something beautiful. They dealt in real estate and had land and mass holdings. One of their problems was holding onto their wealth too tightly. These scoundrel-saints committed the carnal sin of hypocrisy, pretending to be what they weren't, two-faced. They looked one way on the outside but were another way on the inside. Despite how they both pretended to

be on the outside; benevolent, caring, and sacrificing; on the inside, they were greedy, conniving, and selfish.

The two upstanding leaders of the First Church of Jerusalem became two liars. Ananias strolls in with his big bulging bag and lays it on the pile of offerings. He is simply asked by Peter, 'Is this the full income from the sale of the land?' It was sort of a trick question to see if the guy would tell the whole truth. Ananias said, 'Yep.' God said, 'Nope,' and struck him dead for lying. But guess who comes in next? Outwardly beautiful Mrs. Ananias gives a repeat performance, followed by a double funeral within minutes. Many have wondered why God reacted the way He did to these people who are so much like the rest of us.

So as far as we can figure out, God had to teach two lessons, one to the couple and one to the church. He wanted to prevent them from being hypocritical in a world looking for people who behave the way they believe. My guess is that their holding pattern was one nobody wanted to talk about, but everybody did!

Narrative: We know that all this waiting in life is supposed to be good and make us new and improved. But, a lot of the *holding patterns* can be pretty strenuous. So we resist and fight against them; we operate by fear rather than faith; we try to run the other way when we meet trouble. And guess what? We often make the situation harder on ourselves and delay getting what God intends for us. It's a little like horseback riding; if you go with the rhythm of the ride and stride of the horse instead of against them, you have less pain, calluses, and body aches the next day! When we work with and not against the one who creates our *holding patterns*, it may hurt a lot less and help a lot more!

Principle: *Holding patterns* are given to us to make us better. Our cooperation will make the difference in determining the outcomes.
Perspective: Hebrews 12:11 "No discipline seems pleasant at the time, but painful. Later on, however, it produces a harvest of righteousness and peace for those who have been trained by it." (NIV)
Participation: Focus on how a holding pattern made you a better person even though getting through it was tough!

Paul's Conversion (Acts 9)
Background: We now come to one of the most famous portions of the New Testament and a most arresting holding pattern. This is where a guy gets a life change and a name change.

The old guy, Saul, has been on an unrighteous rampage against the new Christians, especially Jews. The nice, neat little Christian community is blown apart by persecution. Saul is still chasin' them; they are like scattering bugs like a beetle from under an overturned rock. It indicates that he was literally breathing down their necks. This guy had to be stopped, and there was only one way to do it; make him blind so he could see God.

Saul made the 150-mile trip in 32 AD from Jerusalem to Syria, where the badgered believers had run for their safety. He was on his way to get the people following *The Way* out of the way. Instead, he would be confronted by the God whose people he was persecuting. Finally, their God had had enough. On the way there, Saul, was knocked off his high horse and fell to the ground, blind as a bat and hearing voices. It was one of the few times in life when he had nothing to say.

He needed someone to lead him to the city, but no one signed up to be killed. Then he met God, who identified Himself as Jesus, the very one he was persecuting. He was told that Ananias would escort him, and his name, Saul, would be changed to Paul. And get this, the man with the new name will switch sides, sign with God's team and go into the world to make the game plan happen. Then, of course, the Jews would be thrilled and give him a send-off party, congratulating him on his promotion. (Not Likely!) It took three days of blindness and fasting to allow God to tell him what he would do and what would happen to him. Funny thing, Paul was going to be persecuted! (What goes around comes around.) So this holding pattern is a no-brainer.

Narrative: There's a saying; it is always darkest before the dawn. In life, it sometimes seems like things get more complicated, more complex, and more intensive before they improve. Compare this to the birth of a child. The author of this book knows zero about this, at least from personal experience, but my wife tells me that the pain is worst preceding the actual delivery of the baby. The good news? The best comes right after the worst.

Principle: Some *holding patterns* have a way of getting harder just before they get easier.

Perspective: II Corinthians 4:17 "These troubles and sufferings of ours are, after all, quite small and won't last very long. Yet this short time of distress will result in God's richest blessing upon us forever and ever!"

Participation: Name the holding pattern in your life where it seemed darkest before dawn. Explain what things were happening. How did it feel, and what did you learn?

Peter's Imprisonment (Acts 12:1-7)
Background: Another guy out to get the church? Herod the Great, who killed John the Baptist, and James, the brother of Christ, wanted to get in good with the Jews by getting rid of Peter. We can bet it was a noisy arrest, especially since Peter was a Roman citizen. So here is the imprisoned Peter with 16 guards on security detail, four for each of the four watches of the night. He was chained to two guards. One stood at the entrance to the jail itself. This was a big catch; they weren't about to let him get away!

Wouldn't you expect a guy falsely arrested and second-guessed to be complaining, lamenting, demanding his rights, and a lawyer? But singing? That wouldn't have been on the Family Feud board under the category of *things people do when they are in jail!* But that's what he did; nice and loud as only Peter could. No doubt this was getting on the nerves of his cellmates, who were cursing and lamenting. But there was something more unusual than a singing inmate. It was the way he escaped.

Given that he was guarded, he wouldn't get a key from the warden. He was going to need divine intervention. And that's exactly what he had, the God of Abraham, Isaac, and Jacob, the impossibility specialist specializing in rescue efforts. Israel from Egypt and the Egyptians, David from Saul, Daniel from the Lion's Den, Mary, Joseph, and Jesus from Herod. (And that's just for starters.) He knew precisely when and where to show up at a Jerusalem jail where His newest recruit was beltin' it out. You can just imagine the faces of the guards and inmates and the jailer who saw Peter released from his chains, get up and walk out a free man. What? One of God's ministering angels carried out the escape. His God did the impossible; He made a way when there was no other way.

Narrative: Everything that happens to us comes in one of two ways. Things others do to us; things we do to ourselves. Example from childhood: It wasn't your fault the entire class had to stay after school and write 'We don't push people in the lunch line' 200 times. A lot of us do the same thing more than once. Fortunately, God does not reserve His help just for those who only make a mistake once.

Principle: *Holding patterns* may involve circumstances we did not cause ourselves.
Perspective: I Peter 3:17 "Remember, if God wants you to suffer, it is better to suffer for doing good than for doing wrong!"
Participation: You may have faced difficult circumstances due to things you didn't cause. How was it more difficult knowing you didn't cause them?

Paul and Silas in Jail (Acts 16:25-27)
Background: Well, if we aren't back in jail again. Only it's somebody else, Paul and Silas. They were behind bars for converting a demon-possessed woman who told fortunes that made her owner wealthy. (It's often about money, isn't it?) So, here we find them, you guessed it, praying and singing. But, this time, God doesn't send an angel to shake things up; He allows an earthquake to do that. (Possibly an eight on the Richter scale?) We don't know! But we know it was enough to shake the prison's foundations, causing all the doors to open and the prisoners to escape. (Talk about Jailhouse Rock!)

The jailer, who was soon drawing unemployment, was desperate, even contemplating suicide. As a result of his crisis, he and his whole family became Christ-followers. The miracle put an exclamation point at the end of the message. God uses crisis to bring people to Himself!

Narrative: When I attempt to mature in my faith walk, the devil tries to knock the wind out of me! I ask, Why? The only answer is the Lord saying to me, 'I don't want you to think that you can become independent of me and rely on your own resources.' *Holding patterns* cause me to be more reliant on God; how He wants me to depend on Him, how close He wants our relationship to be, and how much He wants my faith in Him to grow. The holding pattern may be painful but nonetheless productive in my spiritual life.

Principle: A holding pattern's ultimate objective is God bringing people into a closer relationship with Himself.
Perspective: II Chronicles 20:12 "O our God, won't you stop them? We have no way to protect ourselves against this mighty army. We don't know what to do, but we are looking to you."
Participation: Have you had a crisis in your life that brought you closer to God? If so, how are you sustaining this closeness?

The Ephesian Elders (Acts 20:17-38)
Background: The context of this holding pattern is an emotional farewell given by Paul to the elders of the newly-formed Ephesian Church. This city was his headquarters for three years during his third missionary journey. (54-57 AD) It was the highest point of his ministry, resulting in planting several churches within a 100-mile radius. He was convinced this would be the last time he would be with the church leaders. A full re-cap of Paul's career characterized his steadfastness in the sacred task. He's telling the whole truth about the Gospel and their role in leadership in this church. This was in a pagan city of a quarter-of-a-million people who worshiped Diana, the fertility goddess. Her temple was one of the Seven Wonders of the World, which took 220 years to build. His message included an explicit warning about people inside

the church and false prophets seeking to harm the church. Paul called the Judaizers wolves, who would attack church members he referred to as sheep. Here's the connection. He entrusts their young pastor-shepherds to the Chief Shepherd for guidance and protection.

The closing verses of Paul's farewell address are the most moving. He kneeled down and prayed with them. All of them are weeping and in deep sorrow, knowing that most likely they would not see each other again on this side of heaven. It was a moment of abject sadness yet one of great gladness.

The very faith which was part of their lives would assure them of an eternal reunion with the Lord and their friend. A group of young church leaders knew their loss would eventually be the gain of life after death beyond the holding pattern.

Narrative: One of the hardest things in life is having to say goodbye to someone we won't see until heaven, in some cases, never again. Goodbyes are painful; they represent separation from those we love, without whom our lives seem empty. We can be in a holding pattern initiated by goodbye until we can say hello again in the next life. This extends a lifetime; we don't have the option of ending it or simply forgetting it. We have to adjust our lives and live in spite of the loss.

Principle: *Holding patterns* often include the loss of a loved one we won't see again in this life.
Perspective: I Thessalonians 4:13-14 "And now, dear brothers, I want you to know what happens to a Christian when he dies so that when it happens, you will not be full of sorrow, as those are who have no hope. For since we believe that Jesus died and then came back to life again, we can also believe that when Jesus returns, God will bring back with Him all the Christians who have died."

Participation: Identify a holding pattern involving the passing of someone close to you. Do you anticipate seeing this person again in heaven or not? In either case, how are you dealing with this loss?

Paul Brought to Trial (Acts 24:27)

Background: Paul is in a Roman prison. He has been there for two years. (And finally, here comes da' judge!) He is being moved around like a pawn on a royal chessboard where a real king and queen make all the moves. They were sorta' hoping Paul would offer them a bribe like everyone else. (Not just in those days either!) No such luck; he was looking to the Lord, not a human system, to free him. After all, he was free; his captors were in the real prison. We know, too, that the judicial system moved at about the same speed as it does today! (Lord, spare us!)

He's there on trumped-up charges of being a trouble-maker. Yet, he is honored to identify with his Master, who was also put through a false trial on flimsy evidence. The Romans contested that Paul was troubling them by stirring up the Jews with his gospel message. But no matter, they were absolutely committed to putting a stop to it before these small-minded Jews decided to rear up their heads against Romans, whom they hated. The Roman leaders added insult to injury. After two years in prison, they left their well-known prisoner there. But, that is exactly what God had planned.

Here is the New Testament version of Joseph, who also found himself in jail on construed charges. Unfortunately, we don't have any record of how Joseph handled his dilemma, but we see Paul handled it with grace and dignity; he took the high road, didn't fight fire with fire, render evil for evil, counter-attack, or show disrespect. Instead, he acted like the Christ he had met on the road to Damascus. He saw with new eyes and reacted in new ways; he practiced what he preached. And people no doubt noticed; even King Agrippa told Paul he had almost convinced him to become a Christian. (Almost...?)

Paul had no idea what this holding pattern would be in his life. He didn't know if he would ever leave prison; he might just die there. But either way, he was going to be okay with his God and the people who hated and mistreated him, just as they did Jesus.

Narrative: It is not if we have troubles and problems but how we choose to respond to them. We are not expected to do it all perfectly or consistently. After all, we are but mortals who make mistakes. Yet, our faith gives us the capacity and ability to react to human happenings differently from those in our lives who have no one to trust or rely on.

For instance, your neighbor who watches the nightly news is pessimistic and hopeless about where the world is headed and will end up, or your coworker is obsessed with the next world war. And you are the only Christ-follower or church-goer on your block. Oh sure, you worry about things; paying the bills, the kid's grades, your ailing parent, like everybody else.

But you and I have a different attitude regarding the condition and future of civilization as we know it. It's not how things end; it's if we are ready for eternity. We can ultimately be optimistic. But, your neighbor may wonder how many prescriptions you're on and why you're not consumed by panic and fear. So they ask, "What's with you? You don't seem to lose sleep over how things are going!" And as you prepare to answer, you're thinking, 'I'm so glad you asked.'

Principle: *Holding patterns* allow us to behave differently in the face of uncertainty, allowing us to share our hope with others.
Perspective: I Peter 3:15-16a "Quietly trust yourself to Christ your Lord, and if anybody asks why you believe as you do, be ready to tell him, and do it in a gentle and respectful way. Do what is right."
Participation: Was there an instance when you reacted to something differently from others in similar circumstances? Did someone notice or comment about it? Did you have occasion to share the reason for your hope with them?

The Epistles
Romans
Waiting for Closure (Romans 8:19-23)
Background: This New Testament book was written from Corinth. It is a blending of theology and practical application. Chapters 1-12 contain the basic principles of the Christian life. The last four chapters instruct on how to live them out. Paul compares the new life in Christ to an airplane. The old life is our plane on the tarmac, waiting to take off, and the new life is flying above the clouds beyond the gravitational pull of the old life. This describes how believers in Christ should be more under the control of the new nature than the old nature.

This new freedom is courtesy of Christ, who died to give us a new nature. He uses another word picture, a pregnancy, to describe believers waiting for this life on earth to be over. He says people groan in pain like an expectant mother, waiting to be delivered into the new life. He goes as far as to say that God has allowed (not caused) this to happen so that He can deliver people who caused sin, sickness, sadness, and sorrow to exist. This promise came in the third chapter of the first book of Genesis.

This is the record of two people who brought sin into the world and the plan God already had to solve it. The death of God's Son allows us to be joint-heirs with Him forever. Paul's hope for the Romans and the rest of the world is to look beyond the eternal temporary to the eternal. Too, he concludes the chapter by reminding us that nothing can separate us from God's love in Christ.

Narrative: I'm one of those people who can wait forever for surprises. You won't find me sneaking around the house while you're running errands. Nope! For me, anticipation and looking forward to the surprise is half the fun of waiting for it; once you know what it is, the anticipation is over! But ask any mother. They don't miss the painful period of anticipation of childbirth. When we are in the middle of a holding pattern, it helps us look forward to the exciting things that will come into our lives due to the wait.

Principle: Longer *holding patterns* can build excitement and anticipation for what comes at the conclusion, making the wait worth it.

Perspective: Exodus 12:40-42 "The sons of Jacob and their descendants had lived in Egypt 430 years, and it was on the last day of the 430th year that all of Jehovah's people left the land. This night was selected by the Lord to bring His people out from the land of Egypt, so the same night was selected as the date of the annual celebration of God's deliverance."

Participation: Name a more extended holding pattern that made you especially glad when it ended. Can you remember what made it worth the wait?

I Corinthians

Waiting for Healing (I Corinthians 12:6-8)

Background: Paul suffered in another way, a very personal way, with poor eye-sight. But, always the optimist, he chose to view this affliction from a positive perspective. He was grateful for his suffering because it caused him to be very aware of his weaknesses. Up to this point, he had been known as a pagan who did not suffer; but as a convert to Christianity, he suffered a lot! We wonder if he ever regretted his conversion when the going got rough; death threats and intense persecution.

The context of the chapter is Paul's fear of becoming conceited and developing ego problems. This was because he was especially chosen by God, entering the third heaven and receiving special revelations from God. Paul concludes that God has allowed this affliction to keep him from touting his apostolic stardom. The Greek word describes Satan buffeting him like a slap in the face.

His condition is chronic opthalmois. This is the Greek word from which we get ophthalmologist/optometry. It is quite possible it was the result of the damage to his eyes on the Road to Damascus. In addition, it caused his face to be distorted, making him repulsive to those who heard him. This condition may also explain his large handwriting due to the fact that he had unclear vision.

Understandably Paul asks God to take the problem away; he asks Him to do it three times. And God said "no" three times! So Paul finally reasoned that God intended his affliction to make him more useable for some strange reason. The God who made him certainly knew how to fix him! The reason was to remind His sensational servant that he could not accomplish God's mission on his own. So, the reality; was better for Paul to have bad eyes than to have perfect eyesight and not see spiritual things clearly.

This holding pattern was one of many where Paul waited out in his adventurous, tumultuous life. But this one probably brought him the most pain physically and psychologically; he finally realized that he would not see clearly in his lifetime. Thus, this holding pattern conveys a different kind of lesson, one we often lack the spiritual eyes to see.

Narrative: We learn not to ask two questions in a holding pattern. And those are, *why* and *when*? This translates: Why is this happening to me? When does it end? It's hard to see things from an aerial view, as God does. But, God has an overall design for every life and a purpose for everything He allows to come into our lives. And besides the fact, He doesn't tell us the reasons down here. But, He may tell us when we are in eternity with Him.

Principle: Everyone struggles through adverse *holding patterns*; only God knows the reason for their length.
Perspective: Deuteronomy 29:29 "There are secrets the Lord your God has not revealed to us, but these words that He has revealed are for us and our children to obey forever."
Participation: Have you ever argued with God about why He didn't end your holding pattern? Who won that argument?

Waiting for Reward (I Corinthians 15:58)
Background: Corinth was a commercial metropolis of Greece about 50 miles west of Athens. Its population of 400,000 was surpassed only by Rome, Alexandria, and Antioch. Paul stayed there for a year and a half on his second missionary journey and founded a strong church. However, it was a church characterized by disunity, immorality, Christians taking each

other to court, meat offered to idols and served for dinner afterward, and abuse of the Lord's Supper. He also dealt with false prophets who accused him of being a fraud, disorderly conduct at assemblies, misusing sign gifts, and heresies about the resurrection. Other than that, it was just a sweet little country church. Paul addresses all these issues, which took him two letters to do! There actually were three; we lost one! (Not enough postage?)

Although his opponents criticized how he looked and talked, not like the super-apostles, the people trusted him to tell them the truth, and he did! So it is no surprise that he ends his first letter with one of the most significant chapters In the Bible. Here he answers his critics who contest Christ's being raised from the dead. He reiterates that this truth is the very basis of the Gospel itself, which he backs up with eye-witness confirmation. He saw Christ after He rose from the dead, as did a multitude of others. Many of them were still alive when the letter was written 27 years later after the fact. (And 500 people couldn't have been hallucinating at once; after all, it wasn't Woodstock!)

His death was the basis of a new life. It was also the basis of new bodies that would eventually be changed from mortal to immortal. Thus, believers in Christ would celebrate victory over the ultimate enemy, death! Based on his confirmation of faith, believers were challenged to remain true to their faith. Paul put it this way, "Therefore my dear brothers, stand firm. Let nothing move you. Always give yourself fully to the work of the Lord, because you know that your labor in the Lord is not in vain." (I Corthinians 15:58 NIV) In other words, hang in there and keep doing what you should be doing!

Narrative: What's that old saying, when the cat's away, the mice do play? Well, when Paul was away, the Corinthians went astray! (And, aren't we all a little like the Corinthians?) When we were kids, we remember doing this when we thought no one else was looking. God gives each of us a conscience, a human alarm clock, to let us know when we're about to go into a no trespassing zone. Our conscience is actually the Holy Spirit who comes into our life at conversion. He helps us to resist sin by sounding the alarm.

But when we hit the snooze button and ignore the warning, we get into a heap of trouble. God cares enough to warn us about what hinders us from becoming spiritually mature. But the spiritual alarm system only works if we don't turn it off and go back to sleep!

Principle: *Holding patterns* test our resolve to remain steadfast in our beliefs and strive to live righteously.
Perspective: I Thessalonians 5:19 "Do not smother the Holy Spirit."
Participation: Identify an instance when you ignored your conscience. What was the outcome? Where do you need to be more attentive to the warnings of the Holy Spirit in your life?

Waiting by Helping Others (II Corinthians 1:5-6)
Background: Not all of Paul's suffering was from his physical condition and what his enemies did to him. He was imprisoned, flogged, exposed to the cold, stoned, shipwrecked at night, endangered by bandits, and going without food and clothing. But he also describes dealing with the church and church people and the daily pressures of being a pastor; it was a daily grind. Thus, suffering is the theme of the first chapter of his second letter to a church in constant trouble.

Paul almost lost his life in Ephesus, where the letters were written. He experienced the ultimate suffering when he died some 30 years later in a Roman arena. He identified a holding pattern in this letter; he and those who would come after him would literally suffer through the course of life. But here is an essential lesson that taught us how to go through it. He urges the Corinthian readers to use their struggles to empathize with the struggles of others.

Narrative: It has been said that sympathy tries to understand someone else's trouble; empathy identifies with it because someone has gone through the same struggle. No one goes through every life crisis in the same way. Sometimes we wonder why we go through problems and challenges. But we often discover that someone else has gone through the very same situation. We share something in common with them. Our pain becomes productive when we can empathize with another person.

Principle: *Holding patterns* afford us our chance to learn from a crisis and help others go through theirs.
Perspective: Hebrews 5:8-9 "And even though Jesus was God's Son, He had to learn from experience what it was like to obey when obeying meant suffering. It was after He had proved Himself perfect in this experience that Jesus became the Giver of eternal salvation to all those who obey Him."
Participation: Explain a holding pattern you experienced that allowed you to help another person work through their crises.

Waiting During Persecution (II Corinthians 4:8-9)
Background: In this chapter, Paul has suffering and death on his mind; those who suffered at the hand of those who disbelieved. Paul attempted to bring perspective and hope to his Christian colleagues by stating, "We are hard-pressed on

every side but not crushed; struck down but not destroyed." II Corinthians 4:9 (NIV) The guy who is the non-complainer is also the ultimate optimist. His outlook on the two subjects is based on two realities. First, the power of God in Christ can be clearly seen in suffering. He says that we have this treasure in clay pots that let the light and truth of God leak out when broken. (I like to say God does His best work with cracked pots.) Secondly, that suffering causes the believer to keep their focus on being more excited about what's coming up!

Paul reminds his reader that it will be hard now, but it will be much easier in heaven. His focus is on the invisible more than the visible. After all, when we give our life to Christ, eternal life begins at that moment! Thus, believers are already part of a life that lasts forever in a new heaven and a new earth.

Narrative: Modern society seems mesmerized by NOW! In a cancel-culture; we try to do away with the past, and the fragile condition of the world makes us wary of the future. And we don't like pain; we are conditioned to avoid it and find ways to escape it. Naturally, that affects the way we wait. But the believer has an alternate perspective when it comes to this dilemma. We must condition ourselves to think of the long-term positive effects of our wait. God wants us to look beyond the now and focus on the then.

Principle: *Holding patterns* have more purpose when viewing our circumstances from the long-range eternal perspective than the immediate temporal one.
Perspective: I Peter 1:6-7 "So be truly glad. There is incredible joy ahead, even though the going is rough for a while down here. These trials are only to test your faith and see whether it is strong and pure. It is being tested as fire tests gold and then purifies it, and your faith is far more precious to God than mere gold; if your faith remains strong after being tried in the

test tube of fiery trials, it will bring you much praise and glory and honor on the day of His return."

Participation: As a Christ-follower, what excites you most about eternity with God? How does that help you get through your everyday life?

Galatians

Waiting for the Right Time (Galatians 1:18, 2:1-2)

Background: Paul waited three years until after his conversion on the Damascus road to return to Jerusalem for the first time and 14 years to return the second time. The Judaizers accused Paul of not publishing the true gospel since he wasn't one of the 12 original disciples and had heard the gospel from others. He clarifies in his letter that he did not simply hear it from other men but from God Himself. Perhaps the first delay was for him to become familiar with the gospel. After all, it had been given to him through the direct revelation of Jesus Christ. Perhaps it took him that long to get up the courage to meet Peter, the lead disciple and most influential leader in the Christian community.

Paul couldn't stay too long because of the potential reaction of the ever-hostile rabble-rousers who would have run him out of town. So instead, the disciples of Christ who accepted and supported him, supplied him with a safe trip to Caesarea, from which he sailed to Tarsus, his hometown. Paul did not become a superstar overnight; he went home to wait.

Fourteen years later, he returned to the capital city, Jerusalem. He went there for three reasons. The first confirmed that he was still preaching the right gospel, underscored by the continual persecution against him. Second, he defended his position on Gentile circumcision, something the Judiazers had demanded of the Christian converts insisting they must become Jews before becoming Christians. (How confusing was that?) Third, he was to confirm the great work done by preaching the gospel to the Gentiles, one he didn't want undone by the jealous Jews who wanted these people more devoted to the Law than to the Lord. Paul also took two interns with him, Barnabas and Titus.

Before returning, the two holding patterns that preceded his trip to Jerusalem were forecasted. (See Ephesians 3:3) Part of Paul's wait was to be appointed by the church at Antioch, the first place the believers were called Christians. He became their official delegate and represented their case against circumcision.

Narrative: Ever have one of those 'aha' moments when you ask, "Why does this seem so familiar?" A divine déjà vu? Is history repeating itself? This can happen with *holding patterns.* The longer our life, the greater the chances of duplications, a repeat of life experiences. If we fail to learn from the first go-around, God may repeat the process until we learn what He intended us to know.

Principle: *Holding patterns* often correspond with each other to help us learn all God has to teach us.
Perspective: Romans 5: 2-4 "For because of our faith, He has brought us into this place of highest privilege where we now stand, and we confidently and joyfully look forward to actually becoming all that God has had in mind for us to be. We can rejoice, too, when we run into problems and trials, for we know that they are good for us; they help us learn to be patient. And patience develops strength of character in us and helps us trust God more each time we use it until finally our hope and faith are strong and steady."

Participation: Have you ever had to repeat a holding pattern to learn what God intended for you to know? What did He teach you?

Waiting for Correction (Galatians 6:7-9)
Background: This epistle was written to the Galatians, descendants of the Gauls who later became Frenchmen. Paul, the author, had visited their hometown on three of his missionary journeys between AD 45 and AD 54.

At the end of the third journey, he wrote the letter in Ephesus shortly before writing his letter to the Romans. In this writing, he addresses the infiltration of Jewish legalists determined to stamp Christianity with a Jewish trademark. They were intent on enslaving the free Gentiles to the religious rules of the law. This law-vs-religion system requires us to keep the law to earn a relationship with God by one's *works* instead of trusting the *work* of Christ.

Paul explained that the law prepared the way for the Lord who completed it. The law didn't save people from sin but simply showed them their sin, from which Christ redeemed them. Using the metaphor of enslaved people and the freemen, he showed them that they were no longer enslaved to the law but freed by the Lord, who adopted them as sons and daughters. They were seeking counsel from the wrong people. Paul attempted to set them straight and get them back on track. Yet, he expresses his great surprise at how quickly these believers were led away from the truth he had taught them. This became an extended holding pattern where the disciples learned to trust in the Lord rather than the law.

He underscores the principle of the Holy Spirit, who was now able to indwell them because of the completed work of Christ;

this would be evident through the fruit of the Spirit manifested in their daily life.

The length of the holding pattern was unknown to them. They didn't know that within 16 years, the religious center of Israel and Christianity would be destroyed. Many of them would die at the hands of pagan Roman rulers who were hostile to those having any other god but Caesar.

Narrative: One of the hardest things for human beings is to ask for help. Seeking is fundamental to health in every aspect of our life. By our fallen nature, we are independent, obstinate, and stubborn. Why else do you think the Bible describes us as sheep? Embarrassing, isn't it? Remember, it isn't wrong to have a need; it is wrong not to get help. There is no shame in weakness. When we are in a hard place, we need God's help and the help of others the most!

Principle: When going through *holding patterns*, we need to seek counsel from people we can trust who will urge us to live by the principles that guide our lives.
Perspective: Hebrews 3:13-14 "Speak to each other about these things every day while there is still time so that none of you will become hardened against God, being blinded by the glamor of sin. For if we are faithful to the end, trusting God just as we did when we first became Christians, we will share in all that belongs to Christ."
Participation: Identify two people you trust to counsel you during a time of waiting in your life. Has someone sought you out? If so, how were you able to help them?

Ephesians

Waiting for Clarity (Ephesians 1:11-14)

Background: Paul did not want two churches, one Jewish and one Christian. He wanted *one united* church. This concern motivated this letter to the Ephesians. They belonged to a luxurious and licentious church where new converts were heavily influenced by the religion of Eastern mysticism, sorcery, and magic. He spends three chapters presenting their position in Christ written from his Roman imprisonment, arguing against cultural religion. The following three chapters present an argument against believers who compromised their faith in the realm of daily life. (Immoral sexual practices connected with the goddess Diana, for instance.)

The first group was those attempting to mislead and confuse them about their beliefs. The second group was trying to confuse them in terms of their behavior. The two were linked. If they were tentative about who Christ was and His truth, they would be tentative about living out the principles of His teaching. It was a New Testament version of it doesn't matter what you believe; you can live as you please.

If Paul emphasized that God had chosen them in Christ before the world began, they could be sure He had saved them. As a result of choosing them, they were marked by the Holy Spirit. (Similar to a cattle brand but much more crucial, permanent, and attractive!) As a result, Christ would own them and make good on His promise to reward them. He also used a banking term. The mark of the Holy Spirit was like a deposit or a down payment on a house. It guaranteed taking occupancy at the right time.

The Ephesians didn't know how long they would have to wait before they cashed in on the inheritance they would receive from believing in Christ. The down payment on their eternal home had been made, but they would not move into the house for a long time! So likewise, all believers are waiting for a move-in date. Christ told His followers that He was preparing a place for them, a house with many rooms, but He didn't tell them when they would be available.

History records that this prominent church closed down before the end of the century. Their holding pattern was shortened, but for the wrong reason, they deserted their faith. As a result, they lost their first love and fell from a place of influence, as John described them in Revelation, chapter two.

Narrative: Remember, God loves you and has a wonderful plan for you to succeed in life; Satan hates you and has a terrible plan for you to fail. Sometimes the enemy has us right where he wants us, maybe giving up on God or our faith. That's what our enemy wants us to do; to give up on God when we need Him the most.

Principle: The purpose of a holding pattern is for our faith to be strengthened, not weakened.
Perspective: II Peter 3:18 "But grow in spiritual strength and become better acquainted with our Lord and Savior Jesus Christ. To Him be all glory and splendid honor, both now and forevermore."
Participation: Which holding pattern allowed your faith to grow the most?

Waiting for Maturity (Ephesians 2:1-10)
Background: Paul underscores the believer's position in Christ, reminding them of what they used to be before they met Him; it wasn't pretty. The word *but* in verse four is the hinge between the old and new life. He reminds them that Christ has saved them. Yet a responsibility went along with it, the *working*

out their salvation. Part of what He will do is seat us in heavenly places with Him. What did God mean when He made this promise? It symbolizes our eternal life, which has already begun.

Thus, Paul simply wants his spiritual children to live differently in a world they are called and commissioned to reach. It also allows them to realize their full potential to walk into the fulness of what He has empowered and equipped them to do. Paul says in Ephesians 2:10, "For we are God's workmanship, created in Christ Jesus to do good works which God prepared in advance for us to do." (NIV) When He says we are His workmanship, He says we are His poem, one to be read by others. Paul hopes believers will make the right choice and live the right way, then and now!

Narrative: If church people today profess to be Christ-followers but, in practice, don't live any differently than anyone else, why would others want what we have? Christ wants His followers to have a different identity, outlook, lifestyle, and hope than everybody else!

Principle: *Holding patterns* allow us to demonstrate the power of the one who is making us different so we can make a difference in the lives of others.
Perspective: II Corinthians 5:17 "When someone becomes a Christian, he becomes a brand new person inside. He is not the same anymore. A new life has begun!"
Participation: How would people know that Christ has made a difference in your life? If so, how is that confirmed?

Phillippians

Waiting for Endurance (Phillippians 1:6)

Background: Philippi was the first of the European churches in what is now Greece, where Dr. Luke had been the pastor for six years and where the jailer was among the first converts. Paul wrote again from prison, which always added urgency to his message, most likely dictated to Timothy.

He didn't know how much time he had; the churches didn't know how long they had. This was one of his strongest church plants, one free of doctrinal and practical problems, unlike some of his other prison epistle churches. He is writing to commend them for their gift to finance his missionary work. He encourages them to continue to emulate Christ, especially in the good ways they treated each other.

He uses the metaphor of a runner in a race who keeps his eye on the goal and the prize at the end of the competition and keeps going in the right direction. In the selected text, Paul reiterates a promise that the good work the Philippians were doing would be completed on the day of Christ Jesus, i.e., the time of His return. It was not how long they had to wait but the condition of their heart and mind as they waited.

Sadly, history records that this church did not survive much longer. Today, there are only ruins where the city once stood. Yet, we will always be indebted to this Grecian church which modeled the ability to live amid challenging circumstances because of their confidence in God.

Theirs was to be the inner condition of joy, constant and unchanging. On the other hand, happiness depended on how things went outwardly. One could have joy if and when they were not happy! God bestowed inward confidence, stability, and peace through the Holy Spirit. It was then possible for the

Philippian church to have joy in the midst of waiting, a condition only God could give His followers.

Narrative: People often base their happiness and fulfillment on what's happening outside: The stock market, a new steak house, their kids getting all A's, a bigger house, a 75-inch TV, or if your team made the World Series. Their focus is less on the inside. Do I have peace with the important people in my life? Am I content with what I have? Is stress consuming me? Let's say that when a marriage falls apart, or a kid goes AWOL, it won't matter what size TV you have!

Principle: Surviving a holding pattern is based on the strength of our spirit inside, not on the circumstances outside.
Perspective: II Corinthians 4:16-18 "That is why we never give up. Though our bodies are dying, our inner strength in the Lord is growing every day. These troubles and sufferings of ours, after all, are quite small and won't last very long. Yet this short time of distress will result in God's richest blessing upon us forever and ever. So we do not look at what we can see right now, the troubles all around us, but we look forward to the joys in heaven which we have not yet seen."
Participation: Was there a time in your life when you based your happiness on what was happening *externally* more than the inner condition of your spirit *internally*? What did your holding pattern look like during this time?

Colossians
Waiting for Hope (Colossians 1:5-6)
Background: The Colossae Church was about 100 miles east of Ephesus, near the border of Asia. It was represented on the Day of Pentecost, making it an essential outpost of gospel witness. It made another of Paul's prison epistles more important. His letter was motivated by a concern for a

dangerous heresy making significant headway in this young congregation. Under the guise of higher thought or secular philosophy, it was a mixture of Greek, Jewish, and Oriental religion teaching that angels were the bridge between God and man. Later it became what was known as Gnosticism, teaching that Christ was not God in the flesh.

In his writing to the Colossian Church, Paul again reiterates fundamental Christian doctrine. His two-fold message: Christ is superior to angels because He made them, and Christ was sufficient to be the go-between for God and man. He did not need any substitutes, not Mary or angelic beings. Like the Ephesian letter, he presents true belief as the basis of matching behavior and addresses the need for holy living and right relationships. This admonition was incentivized by the hope of Christ's return, the basis of their worldwide witness, and their new way of life to back it up. Simply, their hope for the future determined how they lived in the present.

Narrative: Hope in the future sets followers of Christ apart from those who don't have the same hope. The world is a hostile, pessimistic place to live where people figure they only get one life on the planet. They have no hope beyond it. And subsequently, no consequences for how they live. This is part of our modern-day thinking. There is no God, ultimate authority, or accountability for how we live our lives. If people think that their life on earth is the only one there is, they have to get it all crammed into a few fleeting years. Our modern mantra is, 'You only go around once; get all the gusto you can get.' On the other hand, believers know there is a God, the ultimate authority to whom they are accountable and with whom they will spend eternity. Thus, they have hope in a hopeless world.

Principle: Waiting is facilitated by optimism based on the assurance that this is not the only life there is.
Perspective: Ecclesiastes 3:11 "Everything is appropriate in its own time. But though God has planted eternity in the hearts of men, even so, many cannot see the whole scope of God's work from beginning to end."
Participation: How does it help you to know that this life is simply preparing you for the next one?

Waiting for the Right Choices (Colossians 3:1-4)
Background: Paul tells his readers they should set their minds on heavenly things, not earthly things. (Not easy to do!) In other words, if you profess to be identified with Christ, you live the way He lived, taught, and modeled for His followers. When He returns and comes to get His church at the end of the world, we will appear with Him in glory. He compares this behavior to clothing. The old life represents the old clothes; the new behavior symbolizes the new clothes. The word picture could be a person coming in after a day of working on the farm and changing into a tuxedo or an evening gown to attend the opera. (No one would think of wearing work clothes to a gala event, would they?)

In a sense, Paul tells his readers to dress up in new deeds, which Christ has equipped them to do. The book of Revelation, chapter 19:8, talks explicitly about believers at the judgment, wearing the works they have done. (It might be a bit drafty for some of us.) This is how they show off for God, letting the world see the difference Christ has made in their lives.

He also tells them how they are to treat each other in the community of faith, their spouses, parents, children, and employers. They were to do their work as if the Lord was their boss, to do it as a ministry and not just a job. Ministry is not just reserved for pastors. This is part of the spiritual apparel they are to put on; they are to make a faith fashion statement and make their divine designer look good. The Colossians got the message; they lived distinctly from everyone else as they waited to see the Lord at His appearance.

Many Christians in the first century believed that Christ would come back in a generation, at least by the year AD 100! So, they figured they could hold on until then. But, when this did not happen, many of them gave up on their timetable or gave in; the holding pattern was too long for them. So, they traded in their tuxedos for their dirty work clothes.

Narrative: One of the distinctives of being human is having a will and making choices. Animals have the same capacity. Just ask me about Rascal, my dog, but the consequences are not as critical. It helps to remember that *holding patterns* are designed to improve us. When we choose the right way to get through our holding pattern, we not only enrich our life now but also enter eternity richer in the rewards God gives us.

Principle: During our *holding patterns*, we are to make good choices that affect our preparation for Christ's return.
Perspective: Revelation 19:7-8 “Let us be glad and rejoice and honor Him; for the time has come for the wedding banquet of the Lamb, and His bride has prepared herself. She is permitted to wear the cleanest and whitest, and finest of linens. Fine linen represents the good deeds done by the people of God.”
Participation: What behaviors do you feel are most important for a believer in anticipation of eternity with Christ?

I Thessalonians

Waiting for the Fulfillment of God's Promise

(I Thessalonians 4:13-18)

Background: In this earliest of the epistles, the first letter deals with the two topics of the Second Coming of Christ and the gathering of His saints. This information was vital for these believers who had two fears. One, those who were already dead would miss the Second Coming. Those living on earth would be left behind and miss the reunion party.

Paul assures them that the people who went before them weren't dead. They were simply asleep, a term that affirms death is only temporary in the scriptures. It is an interim between dying and coming alive again. People who are asleep don't stay asleep; they wake up. It's a term Jesus used to describe Jairus's daughter. He instructs them not to sorrow, at least not to sorrow like everyone else who has no hope of life after death. They have a different kind of sorrow because they have a different kind of hope. The distinct hope is based on the resurrection of Christ preceded by the resurrections which God performed throughout the scriptures.

Paul describes the wondrous reunion between those already dead and those still alive. "For the Lord, Himself will come down from heaven with a mighty shout and with the soul-stirring cry of the archangel and the great trumpet-call of God and the believers who are dead will be the first to rise to meet the Lord, then we who are still alive and remain on the earth will be caught up with them in the clouds to meet the Lord in the air and remain with Him forever." I Thessalonians 4:16-17 (NIV) Many refer to this event as the *Rapture* based on *rapteo*, the Greek word for taken up. The dead and the living will be drawn to heaven like metal to a magnet.

The question, of course, was when is this supposed to happen? Paul doesn't know, so he doesn't say. All he knows is that it *will* happen. He urges them not to calculate when Christ is coming but to focus on the hope of the actual event. This helps them not spend all their time grieving, interfering with their daily living. This would be just what the Devil and the false teachers wanted; a life lived in fear, not faith! What is central to their situation is that the wait will have a happy ending, however long it takes. Those who have died and are yet alive in Christ will live forever in heaven. Word to the wise: When it comes to the return of Christ, it's not *when* but how we live until *then*!

Narrative: Many of us don't have a holding pattern on our bucket lists. If we do, we prefer to feel happy and have things go the way we want them to, but living in a permanent amusement park where you get on the rides with a Fast Pass isn't likely to happen. Life situations confirm that reality. And besides, we wouldn't appreciate the sunshine as much if we didn't have a few rainstorms. And if we lived in a tension-free bubble with no problems, we wouldn't be as excited for the Lord to come back and make everything perfect! As the songwriter says, "If we didn't have any problems, we wouldn't know that He could solve them!" So then, every holding pattern will have a happy ending in eternity. All that waiting will pay off big time! However, we don't go from paradise here to paradise there!

Principle: Christ who came the first time will come the second time, guaranteeing that all life's *holding patterns* will have a positive outcome.

Perspective: II Peter 3:13 "But we are looking forward to God's promise of a new heaven and a new earth afterwards, where there will be only goodness."

Participation: Perhaps you've had a holding pattern that didn't end happily. But imagine how much better the outcome will be when Christ returns. Why is that?

II Thessalonians

Waiting for Something to End (II Thessalonians 2:1-3, 7-10)

Background: This second letter to the Thessalonians was written in AD 52, weeks after the first letter. Paul explains that the Day of the Lord comes only after the great apostasy and turning away from God. But unfortunately, he was not in Thessalonica long enough (only three weeks) to instruct the church about these things, so he had to do it by another letter. Moreover, he had been run out of town by his adversaries, the same ones who persecuted the Thessalonians who stayed strong in suffering.

This made the subject matter of these letters even more critical. These tried and true folks wanted to know when the Lord was coming back, something that would shorten their suffering. He explains that the Lord's imminent coming was not immediate. Bad guys were trying to scare these young Christian believers into thinking that the Lord had already come and canceled their airlift. The apostasy that comes before Christ returns would be called the *falling away,* when the antichrist, the man of sin, rules the world. Neither one of these events would happen during the first century.

Paul points out that the spirit of the antichrist was already present, but the new leader had not yet appeared! This person was yet to show up many centuries later. The Antichrist would be what his name implies; he would be against God and pretend to be Christ. Like the Evil One who seduced humankind into sin by setting himself up as an alternative god, Satan will empower the Antichrist to do miracles, deluding many people only in a different age.

Yet amidst this dismal forecast, there is one bright spot. The Christian Church made of Christ-followers would hold off the coming of the apostasy and the antichrist for quite a while; it would be a *restraining force against evil* in an age of lawlessness. The metaphor of the Grand Coulee Dam gives us a word picture of what this looks like. The spiritual dam is removed, and the floodwaters of evil are unrestrained. This happens when Christ takes the church out of the world at the Rapture, and all the forces of evil submerge the earth. Satan will use the false god trick to deceive people into believing in and following him instead of the true God. (Just like in Eden!) The question is the same: How long will the church be in the world before it is taken out? Obviously, that event didn't occur between AD 52 and the end of the first century. It is yet to happen.

These first believers thought the same thing; that the return of the Lord had already taken place, and they missed it. Some concluded they could live the way they used to, precisely what the great deceiver wanted them to do. He didn't want the dam in place. He wanted it removed so he could flood the world with wickedness!

Narrative: Being in a holding pattern does not excuse us for giving up on God or giving into evil. The Thessalonians didn't, and we shouldn't either! Living this life is not all about us. It is about its impact on other people. It includes our family, neighbors, the company we work for, our friends and enemies, and the people we pray for. Why? Because whether we know it or not, the things we say and do affect them in some way, good or bad. This is especially true when you and I are going thru tough times, when things go wrong, when we're disappointed and when we make mistakes. People see us up close and personal when they see Christ in us as we attempt to live by His principles in the face of crisis and uncertainty.

Principle: While on hold, we are to be a redemptive force in the world, distinct in what we believe and how we behave, lives that contrast, not conform to the culture.
Perspective: Romans 12:2a "Don't copy the behavior and customs of this world, but be a new and different person with a fresh newness in all you do and think."
Participation: What is one thing you can do to hold back the onslaught of evil in our world today?

Waiting for Instruction (I Timothy 6:17-19)
Background: The letters to Timothy are a part of the Pastoral Epistles written between Paul's first and second imprisonment. They are written to Timothy, the son of a Jewish mother and Greek father. Timothy joined Paul on his second journey. Paul regarded him as a spiritual son. His name meant one of great value. He was also preparing him for the Christian ministry, namely the oversight of the Ephesian church. After Paul visited the Ephesians and the elders, he left Timothy to pastor the congregation.

Much of the first letter to Timothy contains instructions about running the church, including leading worship and selecting church leaders. Paul also gave special personal reminders about his integrity compared to the false teachers (wolves) attempting to disrupt the church and mislead people. He warned them about their love of money, not investing only in earthly things but, more importantly, in eternal things. Paul puts it this way, "Command those who are rich in this present world not to be arrogant nor put their hope in wealth, which is so uncertain; but to put their hope in God, who richly provides us with everything for our enjoyment. Command them to do good, to be rich in good deeds, and to be generous and willing to share. In this way they will lay up treasure for themselves as a firm foundation for the coming age so they may take hold of life that is truly life." I Timothy 6:17-19 (NIV) This was not what affluent church members wanted to hear, especially from some pastor younger than their children! Though they were older didn't mean they were wiser. They missed the point: Don't seek to be wealthy on earth but store up heavenly wealth for eternity. He told them not to hold on to temporary things too tightly. You can't take it with you, but you can send it on ahead!

Narrative: If we live only for the present and not the future, we use things unwisely. All kinds of folks waste and misuse what they have. God wants us to utilize this time and experience to take inventory of what we have and how we're using it; to re-assess our priorities. The entire holding pattern is wasted if we decide not to do this.

Principle: *Holding patterns* prompt us to use and invest our resources wisely, making eternal investments.
Perspective: I Timothy 6:18-19 "Tell them to use their money to do good. They should be rich in good works and give happily to those in need, always being ready to share with others whatever God has given them. By doing this, they will be storing up real treasure for themselves in heaven; it is the only safe investment for eternity! And they will be living a fruitful Christian life down here as well."
Participation: How could you make an earthly investment in the short term which will pay dividends in the long term?

Waiting in a Place of Bondage (II Timothy 1:12)
Background: Paul was once again imprisoned in Rome, where he would become a martyr for the Master who had died for him. Unfortunately, this was during the time when Nero had committed a heinous crime against his fellow Romans, for which he needed to blame someone else. This mood sets the tone for Paul's second letter to his younger pastor appointee, Timothy, to take over the church as Paul prepared for his own death.

One of the greatest pieces of evidence of Paul's security in Christ and maturity in faith was the up-look and out-look he maintained and his focus on the welfare of others more than his own. As he faced death, Paul was resolute in courage, knowing it was inevitable but that he would be graduated to glory. His last instructions to his spiritual son were given against the backdrop of the end time in which he describes the forecast of the church, one coming true before our eyes today! His preview was through the eyes of faith.

In the context of the first chapter, he identifies the reason for his suffering, of which he is unashamed, confident that God is able to guard what has been entrusted to him until the day that Christ returns. In the last chapter of this letter, he also references this when he uses the dual metaphors of running the *race* and finishing the *fight*, knowing that the Lord will reward both with a crown. This eternal perspective directed Paul's earthly pilgrimage amidst being imprisoned and false teachers turning against him. His enemies had already lost; he had already won!

Paul had anticipated his death from the day he was converted, a period of about 35 years. He lived with the constant threat of his enemies doing him in; He had spent his conversion life on the run. His last days were intensive, just as his Master's had been. As referenced in the Old and New Testament heroes of faith, their waiting periods left them exhausted in spirit, emotion, and body. They often felt that something in them had already died, but this only served to make their hope of the next life come to life! And remember, Paul never retired from ministry; it was only ended by death.

Narrative: No one promised *holding patterns* would be fun, especially when God's people faced persecution for being Christ-followers; following the example and experience of Christ Himself. It reminds me of the wall plaque in my study: "Lord, help me remember that nothing will happen to me today that you and I can't handle together. Amen." Yet, we want to give up, just as believers who've gone before us have felt. Although God helps us get through the wait, He doesn't deny us the right to complain, become angry with Him, or become despondent over our situation. God already knows what will happen and how you feel about it, and He hasn't stopped loving or given up on you!

Principle: We can feel like giving in and giving up in these waiting periods. Even though we believe the outcome will be good, we can still feel overcome by fatigue and frustration.
Perspective: Galatians 6:9 "And let us not get tired of doing what is right, for after a while we will reap a harvest of blessing if we don't get discouraged and give up."
Participation: Does this example describe how you feel when you go through your *holding patterns*? How do you choose to work through these feelings in your situation?

Waiting for Victory (II Timothy 2:2)

Background: Part of Paul's instruction to Timothy, the apprentice in training, is to be firm in his faith. He uses the metaphor of a soldier; the word picture is significant for several reasons. It implies that there is a war. Paul knew about warfare. It originated with the war between God and Satan in heaven, one which Satan lost when he was demoted to earth. He entered into war with the human race. This was evident in the attacks upon Paul and the Christians.

Paul took his orders from divine headquarters, from the Commander in Chief of the forces of heaven and earth, Lord Sabaoth. The fight takes place in the course of everyday life. The soldier focuses on fighting undistracted by worldly things and is confident that the ultimate war has already been won though the daily battles must be fought!

No doubt, Timothy asked, how long do I have to be at war? Paul simply expected him to be a soldier, not a Marine in dress blues or a combat soldier in kakis toting a gun. But a spiritual warrior who would put on the whole armor of God, ready to do hand-to-hand combat against the unseen forces of the evil one. His armor would be the Sword of the Spirit, the specific truths of the Word of God, and prayer.

Paul was a veteran warrior who fought numerous spiritual wars in cities where he had preached and founded churches. But, unfortunately, the former Pharisee had friends who hated traitors and considered quirky Christians a threat to their power!

Timothy faced a different holding pattern from any he had previously experienced. War was long-term; it would continue his whole life. We don't always realize that every holding pattern deals with a spiritual conflict. It is instigated by the enemy of our souls who hates God, is revengeful and comes up against him by hurting those he loves. The conflict is one we are called and commissioned to fight every day until The Day of Christ when He overcomes His ultimate enemy. Christ has won the war, but Christians must fight the battles in His power and artillery. No wonder *holding patterns* are hard, and waiting is wearisome. They are war zones. However, only one-third of the angels fell from heaven with Satan. Two-thirds remained there to help God's people win the victory over sin; they outnumber the bad ones two to one! Our God claims victory over the Evil One.

Narrative: Christians learn that wars are not only fought in foreign countries by an army or a navy. Our war is with unseen forces attempting to keep us from either knowing Christ or growing up into maturity in Christ. Face it; there are a lot of so-called Christ-followers who are losing their battles. They break the rules and wonder why they can't win the game. It's our choice whether we win or lose. We must understand that we are in a war with a real enemy with the armor (protection) and ammunition (power) to win it!

Principle: *Holding patterns* can involve spiritual warfare in life. Our faith equips us with the power to overcome the Devil and his evil forces.

Perspective: Ephesians 6:13 "So use every piece of God's armor to resist the enemy whenever he attacks and when it is all over, you will still be standing up."

Participation: How has your faith in Christ helped you deal with spiritual warfare in your life? Explain how you can claim victory in spiritual conflict.

Waiting for Change (Titus 2:12,13)

Background: This tiny but loaded letter was written close to when Titus became a pastor in Crete, the island of one hundred cities and the legendary birthplace of the Greek god Zeus. Cretans were bold, lusty, intimidating, and crude people. Paul labels them liars, evil beasts, and slow-bellied, i.e., lazy gluttons. (Not the kind of people you hope move next door!)

Titus, another of Paul's spiritual sons, was in charge of the Cretan Church. Paul had experience with a church like this when he was on-site with the Corinthians; both had multiple problems. He knew how to take care of a disrupted church, big time! In the selected passage, Paul admonishes the Cretan Christians and their leaders to live out what they had learned, not be controlled by their old nature, but by their new nature; to live godly, not ungodly lives. The incentive: Christ was coming back. They didn't know when, of course, but they knew they were supposed to live differently in the present because they had a different future than the non-believers. They were to be alert, not lazy.

They were challenged to live like a set-apart people, showing the world an alternate way to live. They were to model the Master in world views, morals, values, life principles, and daily choices. Paul tells Titus to teach these things and not let people put him down or question his authority because he was a young man. It was a challenging assignment and a hard sell. Getting these folks to live contrastingly in Crete was a difficult and demanding task.

They were called to act like citizens of God's kingdom. They were to give people a sneak preview of the coming kingdom and what a life with the King looked like.

Narrative: Have any of us reached the point in life where we are too old to change? Some of us figure that what people see is what they get; we are just the way we are, and folks will just have to get used to it; self-improvement is over-rated. Our whole life is an ongoing conversion, being changed from what we were into what we are meant to be; holy and whole. God loves us too much to let us stay the same! Healthy people don't make excuses. The only people who get by without changing are dead or raptured. And if you're reading this, you're not in either of those categories, so you can still have time to change at any age.

Principle: Our *holding patterns* allow us to turn away from our old life and turn more to our new life through the maturing of our faith.

Perspective: II Peter 3:18a "But grow in spiritual strength and become better acquainted with our Lord and Savior Jesus Christ."

Participation: Do you see yourself handling *holding patterns* more effectively as your faith matures? If so, how? If not, why not?

Waiting for Relief (Hebrews 6:10-12)

Background: The book of Hebrews was God's final message to the Jews. Paul presumably did not write it, but the author did not sign their name. Some say it could have been a woman because of the attention to detail and the descriptive language. Whoever wrote it gave us the letter most correspondent to the presentation of the Law in the Old Testament.

Hebrews was written from the capital city of Jerusalem. This city figured hugely in the life of the people to whom it was written. They were warned about two things; not to forsake their faith and to expect possible persecution if they stayed true to the faith. The opposition would precede it.

Hebrew is like a review before a test covering the basics of why Christ and the new Christian belief system were superior to the law's old legalized system. The Lord, the perfect priest, and perfect sacrifice were superior to the Old Testament law based on imperfect priests and animal sacrifices. The writer warns them not to return to the old because they were persecuted but to remain faithful to their new faith. These frightened Christians were in a holding pattern they didn't see coming. They thought their new faith would be easy, but under pressure, they compromised it for safety and acceptance.

Narrative: We usually don't know the length of our *holding patterns* until after they are over. Throughout the Bible, there were two different patterns. The difference between the two is their length and severity. The impact of the short holding pattern is all at once. The impact of the long holding pattern is spread out over a more extended period of time. So, the shorter ones aren't necessarily easier, but they end more quickly.

Principle: Some *holding patterns* can be shorter than expected and compensate for the longer ones! But both can be equally intensive.

Perspective: Nehemiah 6:14-15 "O my God, I prayed, don't forget all the evil of Tobiah, Sanballat, Noadiah the prophetess, and all the other prophets who have tried to discourage me. The wall was finally finished in early September, just 52 days after we had begun!"

Participation: When did you have a holding pattern that surprised you by being shorter than expected? Was it more or less intensive?

Waiting for Intervention (Hebrews 11:1)
Background: This single verse is the foundation of the entire chapter entitled the New Testament Hall of Faith. It includes 20 different heroes whose fame is centered on their faith; they defied logic and instant gratification. The big names, Cain, Enoch, Noah, Abraham, Isaac, Jacob, Joseph, Moses, Samuel, and David, all passed the faith test. So did the lesser names; Rahab, Gideon, Barak, and Samson. Their faith was truly "the substance of things hoped for and the evidence of things not seen."(KJV) It was a thread that tied them all together, believing the God who promised to reward them even without seeing him. There was another thread in this divine tapestry that tied them together; they would have to wait until the end of time to see the fulfillment of the promise given at the first coming of Christ.

This did not mean that God's People, the church, got all the promises made to the Old Testament believers. (No, sir!) God will fulfill His promises to His Old Testament People, the nation of Israel, *and* the promises to His New Testament people, the Church. Some of them are the same. But the Old Testament people had to have greater faith because they had less history to prove the promises of God to be true. Christians today have all of history to prove them. They see God's track record as outstanding. Thus, every faith hero was in a holding pattern. Each of these God-believing giants has left us a legacy of faith.

Narrative: Normally, grandparents and parents don't outlive their kids. They enjoy leaving a legacy to those who come after them. It can come in the form of money, material things, memories, and instructions that help their offspring get on with their lives. So often, we don't know why we experienced certain things in our lifetime; the generations that follow us will validate them.

These things might include the money we set aside for a grandchild to go to school to become an architect, the baby blanket we made for our own child becomes used by the twins born to our great-great-grandchildren, the china set we received as a wedding present could be used in the White House by a daughter who became the first female US President. God did not intend for us to understand the reasons for everything now.

Principle: *Holding patterns* may not be completed in our lifetime but in the lifetime of those who come after us.
Perspective: Psalm 78:3-4 "For I will show you lessons from our history, stories handed down to us from former generations. I will reveal these truths to you so that you can describe these glorious deeds of Jehovah to your children and tell them about the mighty miracles He did."
Participation: What legacy do you want to leave to those who come after you?

Waiting for Discipline (Hebrews 12:5-11)
Background: Discipline is not something our Lord experienced at the hand of His Father. God does discipline us as His children as our earthly parents do. But, unlike our earthly parents, His motives and methods are always right and in our best interests. (Although it may not always seem that way at the time.) His motive is one of love, wanting us to be the best people we can be. His method is to do whatever it takes to make that happen.

The writer also says that if we believe that our fathers on earth wanted our best, why would our Father in heaven be different? And the writer goes on to explain that we can only grow to be mature people thru discipline.

When God allows us to be in a holding pattern, He knows exactly what He is doing and wants to accomplish through it. Sometimes the discipline is for something we have done wrong for which we need to be corrected. But, often, the discipline is not for anything we have done or failed to do but simply to strengthen our faith.

Narrative: Many of us would just as soon skip this section; it's about discipline. Discipline is the trademark of Christ-followers; discipline is what makes true disciples. Want a weed? Do nothing; let that sucker just grow however it wants to. Want a rose? Attend to it, water, and fertilize it. Time, attention, cultivation, and nurture are all needed to help the rose bush realize its full potential to be healthy and beautiful. So it is with spiritual discipline. That's why the words discipline and disciple are related. What works for plants also works for people!

No one goes thru life without being disciplined in some way by a parent, a coach, a teacher, a drill sergeant, or life itself. Yes, we know it's good for us to have it in the personal and the spiritual realm, but it doesn't mean we understand or like it. Remember when your parent prefaced the discipline with "This will hurt me more than it does you?" And you said to yourself, "Yeah, right," and you wanted to trade places with your parent? We can't always trust our parent's discipline, but we can trust our Heavenly Parent to do it right and for the right reason. He often uses *holding patterns* to teach us new things about ourselves and how we can grow into greater maturity.

Principle: *Holding patterns* often provide a means of discipline, allowing us to realize our full potential.

Perspective: Hebrews 12:10-11 "Our earthly fathers trained us for a few brief years, doing the best for us that they knew how, but God's correction is always right and for our best good,

that we may share His holiness. Being punished isn't enjoyable while it is happening; it hurts! But afterwards we can see the result, a quiet growth in grace and character."
Participation: Identify an area of your life where God disciplined you during a holding pattern. Did it make you a better person? How?

James
Waiting for Stamina (James 1:2-5)
Background: James, the step-brother of Christ, became the lead pastor at the Christian church in Jerusalem. He wrote this small and controversial book. It was presumably written at the close of his 30-year pastorate.

For two reasons, this book had a hard time making it into the New Testament Canon, the standard of acceptance. First, it never mentioned Jesus once. It was like a counterpart to the Old Testament book of Esther, which didn't mention God either. Secondly, it seemed to promote a doctrine of salvation by human works rather than the divine work of Christ.

James practiced what he preached in that his works confirmed Christ's work. In fact, he knew about good works, i.e., he was known by the nickname camel knees because he had calluses on them from praying so much! The focus on living out one's faith was addressed to believers who had been scattered everywhere because of persecution; the foreigners with the funny faith were noticed.

The book is filled with all kinds of practical ways to practice our faith. We could say that James is a New Testament version of Proverbs, asking for wisdom, resisting temptation, using-misusing the tongue, bias toward the rich, worldliness, riches, prayer, and healing. In his opening passage, he challenges his fellow believers to go through opposition for being a Christian with joy! (What was this guy thinking?)

James wants to consider this alternative because testing their faith would develop perseverance and maturity. He says that if they survive the struggle, they will lack nothing. God will provide everything they need to survive and thrive. He reminds them that testing and trials are purposeful and positive. James proved his point painfully; he was stoned and clubbed to death by his opponents not long after this epistle was written. But he truly put his faith to work thru good works and imparted that truth by precept (*what he said)* and practice *(what he did).* He emulated Christ, his older step-brother, big time!

Narrative: As believers, we often ask why the trials and temptations seem to accelerate when we try to grow spiritually and draw closer to God. (You know what I mean?) When we are on hold for whatever reason, we are more vulnerable and easy prey for the enemy. As a result, we learn to hold on to our God more tightly! Remember the hymn, 'This is my Father's world' reminds us "that though the wrong seems oft so strong, God is the ruler yet."

Principle: During our *holding patterns,* we are more vulnerable and susceptible to giving in to temptation.
Perspective: Romans 7:21-22,24a "It seems to be a fact of life that when I want to do what is right, I inevitably do what is wrong. I love to do God's will so far as my new nature is concerned. Oh, what a terrible predicament I'm in!"
Participation: In what ways have you found it hard to do the right things consistently in a holding pattern?

Waiting for Patience (James 5:7-9)
Background: Pastor James continues his faith practicum: Be patient in suffering. (Patient suffering sounds like an oxymoron, like jumbo shrimp.) He is big on this principle because he had to learn it too. Can you imagine losing half your congregation due to re-location, especially under fire from persecution? (Spiritual social distancing: Welcome to Covid-19!)

He compares the Lord's return to the spring and autumn rains. The former represents His first coming and the latter His second coming. As a farmer waits for the rains to water his valuable crops, the Christians are to wait for the latter reign of Christ to bring about a bumper crop of souls as people turn to Him at the end of the world.

The word for patience here denotes mega willpower or self-control. Like many other New Testament people, they believed Christ would come back in their lifetime. Either way, they would have to wait. To put it another way, the gory precedes the glory. That was how it was for Christ, so it is for His followers. James was living and dying proof of this hypothesis for many of Christ's followers in pagan countries.

Waiting is unnatural to our old nature and even to our new one. If we signed on for a holding pattern, we would make sure it was short and sweet, right? But we don't get to dictate our *holding patterns* type, time, or tenure. God, whose Son entered into a holding pattern of the most intense pain and suffering in all of human history, found it anything but short and sweet. Yet, His suffering resulted in the world's salvation. Patience will prove to be productive for all of us, just as it was for Christ. And if God got Christ through His struggle, how will He not get us through ours?

Narrative: You can't read the Bible and conclude that Christ gave His life to make us happy, wealthy, successful, or famous. His goal for us is to become more like Him. Thus, He didn't promise that we wouldn't have tribulation or opposition during our short time on earth. He told us to expect trouble, but He also promised triumph.

Principle: During waiting times, we can develop Christ-like qualities in our life.
Perspective: II Corinthians 3:18 "But we as Christians have no veil over our faces; we can be mirrors that brightly reflect the glory of the Lord. And as the Spirit of the Lord works within us, we become more and more like Him."
Participation: What quality of Christ's character would you most like to develop while you are waiting?

The Prophetical Books
I Peter
Waiting for Testing (I Peter 1:5-9)
Background: We would expect something pretty blunt from the outspoken Peter, wouldn't we? By the time he got around to writing his books, he had mellowed and tempered his temper. But, he never lost his passion for the church of which his faith was foundational. He wrote to a persecuted church, as did James, as evident in places where they were scattered. Emperors of Rome were making life miserable for anyone who was part of The Way and professed allegiance to any other than the king of Rome! The term, fiery trial, describes what the Church members were enduring.

Peter, like James, cataloged a list of behaviors Christ-followers were to put into practice, i.e., distinct living, husband and wife relations, suffering for doing good, needing wisdom, and the role of church leaders. All of this was part of a giant schematic that allowed persecuted believers to look beyond their human dilemma to their superhuman deliverance and live accordingly; other-worldly, if you please.

Peter's instruction is to hold on in hope because their salvation would be completed in the last times. Between then and now, he reminds them that they have an inheritance protected in the present and guaranteed in the future; though tried by fire, their faith would bring great glory to God and confirm their salvation. This was a spiritual coping mechanism based on the three phases of the Christian life: Past-*Justification,* Present-*Sanctification,* Future-*Glorification.* The New Testament people of God are in the middle phase, being set apart unto God. The middle phase is the hardest and the longest. Thus, *holding patterns* are a part of the interim phase, between finding and finishing the salvation process.

Notably, a short time after Peter wrote this work, he and his wife, Concordia, became martyrs. The outspoken disciple and writer gave his life, as did his Master.

James and Peter were present for Pentecost, the church's birthday. They were infused by the power of the promised Holy Spirit, who had turned cowards into stalwart and bold spokespersons for Christ. The latter would die rather than deny their faith and live!

Narrative: It's easy to be a Christian when your life is on cruise control; there are only sunny days, and everything is going your way, right? But then your car has a transmission failure on vacation, you have sun deprivation because of monsoons, or suddenly you feel like you are going the wrong way on the freeway. Then what? Like most of us, your faith idles, your weather report is overcast, and you are looking for the nearest exit. It's hard to be up when everything is going down, and your world is falling in, isn't it? Unfortunately, today's culture tells us we have no other options when this happens but to panic or go into pessimism mode. Still, we have another alternative; we can live a life for Christ because we look forward to a life with Him in a brand new heaven and earth. To put it another way, your outlook depends on your uplook!

Principle: A holding pattern allows us to choose to live out the Christian life on purpose for His purposes.
Perspective: Romans 10:15 "And how will anyone go and tell them unless someone sends him? That is what the scriptures are talking about when they say, 'How beautiful are the feet of those who preach the Gospel of peace with God and bring glad tidings of good things.' In other words, how welcome are those who come preaching God's Good News!"
Participation: As you have lived through your holding pattern successfully, have you ever had the opportunity to share your faith in Christ with someone? What did you share with them?

Waiting for the Next Life (I Peter 2:1-12)
Background: Peter also emphasizes the set apart theme in the second chapter of his first letter. Here he uses the metaphor of aliens and strangers to describe those scattered throughout the world. He challenges them to be pioneers rather than settlers. Pioneers are portable; settlers are stationary. The old hymn says it well, "This world is not my home. I'm just a passin' through; my treasures are laid up somewhere beyond the blue." In other words, they were not to build their mansion here! After all, Peter predicts that someday soon, we will be taken out of the world anyway, so we might as well get used to being here temporarily. Peter takes a lesson from the Old Testament settlers; if you get chummy with the culture, you

will wind up just like them. Then the people of God would lose their influence in their world.

Narrative: Tourists are people who visit a country they don't live in. People who leave one country and move to a new one are called ex-pats or former patriots. This is how it is with a believer who hopes to live in an eternal country. They become ex-pats of earth. They don't get too comfortable and culturally climatized. They don't put their roots down too deeply; they can uproot and move at any time. The balancing act of being in the world but not of the world is not easy, but it can be done!

Life is compared to running a race, a very long race. The Christian life is a marathon, not a 100-yard dash! Everyone will get thru it. Some will finish in the top ten, and some will come in at two a.m. after dark when the race started at noon; others will still be on a break; some will have accidents and pull a hamstring. But they will get thru it.

Scripture also compares life to building a house. Every Christ-follower will build a spiritual foundation based on faith in Christ, but not all will build the same house. Some will build a lean-to, a tool shed; others a condominium, townhome, or a palace. However, He won't force us to make the right choices to live out our everyday life beliefs.

Principle: It's not *do we get thru* a holding pattern but *how we get thru it* that counts eternally.
Perspective: I Corinthians 3:13 "There is going to come a time of testing at Christ's Judgment Day to see what kind of material each builder has used. Everyone's work will be put through the fire so that all can see whether or not it keeps its value, and what was really accomplished."

Participation: How are you doing in your race? How is your home building project going?

Waiting to Triumph (I Peter 5:8-9)

Background: We come to one of my favorite texts in the whole of the New Testament. It talks about Satan attacking us. (Seriously?) I like it for two reasons. One, it reveals Satan for who he is and what he does. Two, it explains how we can defeat him. Satan's name means accuser. Thus, Satan is a prosecutor who attempts to render us a guilty verdict in the world courtroom where Christ serves as our defense attorney. But, unlike any other attorney we know, Christ has pleaded and won our case by taking the penalty of our crimes upon Himself.

Paul describes the Evil One as a roaring lion who stalks his prey and calculates how and when he can strike. He knows his victim's vulnerabilities. This demonic dude may not be very smart, but he sure is shrewd. The devil is described as one who devours us; it sounds like he gulps us down all at once. But the word better translates to render us ineffective, a slow, subtle process. He knows that he cannot take our salvation away; it is permanently purchased and protected by the work of Christ. But, Satan can neutralize its effectiveness when we fail to live it out in daily life.

Both James and Paul offer us a vital strategy to overcome him: 1-Submit to God, 2-Resist the Devil, 3-Draw near God. The first means to depend on God's power and authority. The second means to use the spiritual artillery given us by which to fight the enemy of our souls. The third is to draw closer to God.

As the end of time and the Day of the Lord come closer, we can count on Satan to become more desperate and deceptive because he is running out of time; he will become more blatant and vicious. This is confirmed by the biblical metaphors used to describe the process of his evolution; first, a *serpent*, then a *lion*, and finally, a *dragon*. Note the increase of verocity that characterizes him; he starts subtle and becomes progressively stronger. He is indeed on the lookout for us; we need to be on the lookout for him!

Narrative: One of the realizations we encounter when we hit a holding pattern is that a force is at work behind the scenes. Satan, the ol' devil who got all of us in trouble with our first parents in paradise, is still causin' trouble until he goes into permanent lock-down. He knows how to kick a good person when they are down, distorts their perspective, and accuses them of everything they've ever done wrong. He can even make them think they've lost their faith. (The nerve!) He will do anything and stop at nothing to make a Christian ineffective in living out their faith. After all, they are a threat to his perverted purposes! He tries to take advantage of our vulnerability, especially when we are in a holding pattern!

Principle: *Holding patterns* require that we recognize we are at war with a real enemy who has a customized strategy to defeat us, but we can beat him.
Perspective: Revelation 12:10 "Then I heard a loud voice shouting across the heavens, It has happened at last! God's salvation, power, rule, and authority of His Christ are finally here; for the Accuser of our brothers has been thrown down from heaven onto earth. He accused them day and night before our God."
Participation: Do you sense the Devil is trying to make you ineffective in your Christian life in these final days? Where are you most vulnerable to his attack? How do you defend yourself?

II Peter

Waiting for Discernment (II Peter 3:11-14)

Background: This letter is written within the context of false teachers who challenged the idea that Christ was ever going to return to earth. After all, they contended the Messiah who was predicted to come back was tardy and or just failed to show up. Furthermore, they are convinced that He didn't keep His promises, so they had nothing to worry about; they could forget about living distinctively in a conforming culture.

Peter reminds them that God kept His promise to send a flood to engulf the world, but people just laughed at Noah. Now the people were laughing at Peter for the same thing! God will keep His promise to destroy the world by fire in the future. God is waiting because He wants as many people to find salvation thru Him as possible. He also reminds them that the coming of Christ would come when they least expected it, much like a woman expecting a baby and not knowing when labor will begin. The weary world is pregnant, waiting for the birth of new life in a new world!

Suddenly, like when the rains came and flooded the earth, the firestorms will permanently alter heaven and earth. He challenges them to remember to live the right way; that is the only thing they should be worried about! He instructs them not to second guess God's promises concerning the second coming but live with a confident expectation that it will happen.

Narrative: The age we live in today is much like the age of the first century. False prophets and teachers attempt to mislead God's people by not telling them the truth. Therefore, we need to carefully examine the source and content of what's being taught in many of our churches today. Christ predicted that false teaching would be part of the end times, and even the elect believers would be deceived.

Principle: During *holding patterns*, we need to be careful about what we believe and live according to God's truth.
Perspective: 2 Peter 3:17 "I am warning you ahead of time, dear brothers, so that you can watch out and not be carried away by the mistakes of these wicked men, lest you yourselves become mixed up too."
Participation: How are you able to discern true teaching from false teaching? Why is this important to your Christian life?

Revelation
Waiting for the End Times (Revelation 4:1-7)
Background: God waited for the right time to create the world and then re-created the human race through the redemption of His Son. Christ had to wait to come to earth the first time and is waiting to return the second time. The Holy Spirit waited to enter the lives of believers based on Christ's completed work at the birth of the Church. The Trinity all have been in *holding patterns*!

Let's retrace history. God destroyed the world with a flood and established His people through Abram's call to become the father of many nations. Then He revealed Himself to His people, providing a way of access to Himself through the keeping of the Law. Next, God moved His people into the Promised Land to establish and carry out His mission to the world. He put judges and kings in place to lead them and prophets to warn them of impending judgment and cared for them in captivity. God has always provided a savior figure for His people, the children of Israel. They were never without a leader, guide, rescuer, and a restorer.

Christ was the ultimate savior, different from any judge, patriarch, or prophet. He co-created the world and appeared throughout the generations. He was the perfect sacrifice, dying for the salvation of all people. God knew that there were no human options available to provide salvation. Before time He knew He would send His Son to die for us. This is referenced in Genesis 3:15, the Prolegomena, the Word spoken beforehand. God had already planned to solve the sin problem created by defying God and disobeying His commandments. God is experienced in waiting.

The timing of the first coming had a lot to do with the Jews; they had run out of options. They desired to be ruled by a king like all other nations. (The BC equivalent to keeping up with the Joneses.) It was a wrong decision; they learned that false gods were no replacement for the one and only true God! And all God's judges and prophets couldn't put Israel back together again. First, they were disobedient, then deported, despondent, and desperate. After returning to their homeland, they were made subservient to one power after another. They are yet to be delivered from their holding pattern.

But the timing also had a lot to do with the Romans. They established a one-world government, introduced a common language, and built the finest network of roads to that point in history. They prepared the world for the coming of the Messiah and the Christian Gospel, which would be published to the ends of the known world. Therefore, it was the right time to send the Son, the Savior-Deliverer. This is why Paul quoted God stating that "When the fullness of time had come, God sent forth His Son." (Galatians 4:4 NIV)

God is in a holding pattern, but two things are important to know. One, God is above time but allows Himself to be regulated by it. He knew before time began precisely when He would send His Son into the world both the first and second time, in His own time, just in time!

Narrative: God waited for the world of Roman times to best accommodate Christ coming. He is waiting for the world of modern times to do the same. We live in a modern version of the Roman Empire in an internet world of 2.2 billion computer users worldwide. The Gospel message will be declared to the ends of the earth in a world much larger than Rome. The fulness of time teaches us something very significant about *holding patterns*. Great things come from waiting, which makes the waiting worth it. In actuality, every human holding pattern aims to cause people to know God through Christ and grow in their relationship with Him. Those two residuals are the most important reasons for God to wait. It is often easy to focus on the means and lose sight of the end.

Yes, we want God's ultimate will, but we often don't like the circumstances He uses to realize it. We need to remind ourselves that human sin, suffering, confusion, war, sickness, pain, brokenness, and depravity are all means God allows to work out His purposes. Isn't it amazing that God makes miracles out of messes?

They are temporal means to eternal ends. Thus, our God understands and can empathize with our *holding patterns*. He is intimately familiar with waiting.

Principle: All *holding patterns* are a means of bringing the world into a right relationship with Christ.
Perspective: Acts 17:26-27 "He created all the people of the world from one man, Adam, and scattered the nations across the face of the earth. He decided beforehand which should rise and fall, and when. He determined their boundaries. His purpose in all of this is that they should seek after God and perhaps feel their way toward Him and find Him though He is not far from any one of us."

Participation: Identify ways your *holding patterns* can become what God uses to work out His higher purposes for your life and the people in your world.

Waiting for Protection (Revelation 12:4-6)
Background: This epistle of the apostle John, the beloved disciple of Christ, was written from the isle of Patmos, where he had been banished during the reign and persecution of Emperor Domitian in the late 90s AD. It was as if the beloved disciple was spared the agonizing death all the other disciples suffered. He was an eye-witness in space-time history of all the events at the end of the world. John was given this revelation directly from Christ via a divine messenger. This was not something unusual. Jacob, Joseph, Daniel, and Paul all had visions. John picked up where the prophet Daniel left off; he was allowed to open the book Daniel had sealed five hundred years before.

This was a letter to the seven specific churches that symbolized all the churches throughout history, each awaiting the return of Christ in various stages of spiritual development. The prophecy was directed to the Jews and Gentiles who would confess faith in Christ after the rapture of the church prior to the Great Tribulation. This will be the last seven years before the Day of the Lord is completed. John uses figurative language to describe the literal events which were to take place. It has caused confusion and speculation among those who have tried to interpret it, to say the least! Amidst this tribulation, God promises to protect and deliver His people.

Narrative: Satan has a part in the events of the End Times. He knows his time is running out; his days are numbered. His rule as the prince of this world is about to end.

Nevertheless, he is still mad at God for kicking him out of heaven, and he continues taking out his anger on God's people, the thing he knows will hurt God most. But this false god is no match for the true God who will save His people, immobilize the Devil forever, and create a new heaven and earth eternally.

Principle: *Holding patterns* will become shorter and more intensive as the time of Christ comes closer, but God will cause us to survive.
Perspective: Matthew 24:12-13 "Sin will be rampant everywhere and will cool the love of many. But those enduring to the end shall be saved."
Participation: Does it seem like your *holding patterns* are getting harder in these last days? If so, how do you know?

Waiting for Distinctiveness (Revelation 13:7)
Background: The book of Revelation presents an unholy trinity; Satan, the anti-Christ, and the false prophet; all 100 percent counterfeit counterparts to God the Father, the Son, and the Holy Spirit. Their role is particularly significant in that they try to destroy those who believe in the true God and deceive others, getting them to believe in the false god. They attempt this by doing signs and wonders, just like Christ and His followers, only sourced in Satan's power.

This is inferred by the blasphemy that the unholy trinity uses to bad-mouth God, His truth, and ultimate triumph. Notice that this opposition takes place throughout the world. No believer is exempt.

Because time is running out, the war against us will be accelerated in the days before Christ shows up and takes over!

Therefore, in these final days, we should be aware of false prophets and not trust the false gods of this world.

The scriptures issue a warning to believers not to be misled and deceived. If they are, though they are saved, they will live ineffective and unfruitful lives. They will become part of the problem instead of the solution!

Narrative: Today's church needs to ask this question; if we don't live differently than the world does, why would the world want to profess what we have? Christians are called to be distinct from the culture, not odd but different. They are to be living billboards that advertise the God who created and re-created them!

Principle: This strategic holding pattern reminds us that we are to hold onto and live by the truth, which keeps us from trusting in or living by the standards and practices of the world.

Perspective: II Peter 3:14 "Dear friends, while you are waiting for these things to happen and for Him to come, try hard to live without sinning, and be at peace with everyone so that He will be pleased with you when He returns."

Participation: How is your life as a Christian distinct from everyone else's in these times?

Waiting for Eternity (Revelation 20:1-10)

Background: The Lord's Second Coming is referenced over 300 times in the New Testament and the Millennium six times. Starting with the Rapture, it is a time of universal upheaval represented by the seals, trumpets, and bowls, all metaphors for judgments that will increase in intensity, ultimately affecting the entire world.

All this makes the coming of Christ to rule the world for 1000 years really good news! Numbers are often used as symbols for periods when God does remarkable things. Such is the time of the Millennium represented by the number 1000. It denotes completion. We know for certain that Christ will bring peace on earth and goodwill to men as promised in His birth announcement in Luke 2:14. This is based on His perfectly righteous rule underscored by the absence of Satan and his fallen forces.

Satan's rebellion against God was demonstrated in the attempt to kill Christ at age two and then manipulating God's people to betray and kill Him at age 33. Finally, Satan is bound and thrown into his subterranean jail cell at the Coming of Christ when He sets up His Millennial Kingdom. The text mentions two resurrections, one before and one after the 1000-year reign. The first is for believers, the second for non-believers. What is surprising is that Satan is let loose for a short time at the end of the one thousand years, and still, people will follow him.

Narrative: People today ask where our world is headed and how things will end. Our world will end, but it won't be the end; it will only be a beginning of a re-made heaven and earth inhabited by only those who have committed their lives to Christ and welcome His coming. (Eternal Christmas!) All others who have refused to believe in Him will inhabit the world beneath, called Hell. Everyone will be with God or apart from Him forever; no re-incarnation or second chances.

Principle: The most prolonged holding pattern began before time and will end when time is no more.

Perspective: Hebrews 9:26b, 27-28 "He came once for all at the end of the age to put away the power of sin forever by dying for us. And just as it is destined that men die only once and after that comes judgment, so also Christ died only once as an offering for the sins of many people, and He will come again, but not to deal again with our sins. This time He will come bringing salvation to all those who are eagerly and patiently waiting for him."

Participation: Are you prepared for the end of this holding pattern by knowing where you will spend eternity? How do you know for sure?

Waiting for Heaven (Revelation 21:2-4)

Background: John concludes his dramatic prophecy with a wonderful portrait of a New Heaven and a new earth, the holy city of Jerusalem coming down from Heaven; a place where God will wipe every tear away from His people's eyes, and there will be no more death, no crying or pain.

Narrative: We often wonder what heaven will be like. Will there be long lines to see and talk with the Patriarchs? Will we take harp lessons? Will we have a non-stop worship service? Unfortunately, we don't know much about heaven; we can only imagine. But one thing will be different; sickness, suffering, sinning, sadness, guilt, unforgiveness, war, and injustice will end. We will no longer be fighting, fearful, depressed, lonely, betrayed or forgotten. All of these things will no longer exist.

So making it through all our *holding patterns* with our anxieties, hassles, frustration, and uncertainty will be worth it. As the hymn writer penned it in *It Will Be Worth it All:* "One look at His dear face, all sorrows will erase, so bravely run the race 'till we see Christ."

Principle: Eternity will allow us to see our *holding patterns* in retrospect.

Perspective: Romans 8:18-19 "Yet, what we suffer now is nothing compared to the glory He will give us later. For all creation is waiting patiently and hopefully for that future day when God will resurrect His children."

Participation: Which holding pattern in your life would you most like to have explained in heaven?

THE CERTIFICATION OF *HOLDING PATTERNS*

"When her husband is near and does not let her want for anything she expects, hopes for, and enjoys, a wife says she loves her husband easily and normally. But when the husband is far away, when the waiting is prolonged for months and years, when doubt grows that he will ever return, oh, then the test of love begins."

"What power of real, living, strong testimony emanates from the faithful vigilance, the unquenchable hope which this woman lives behind the bitter doorway of waiting!"

"Oh, how each one of us would like to be the bridegroom who returns disguised as a poor stranger, whom she does not recognize, but to whom she repeats, again and again, her certainty of his return and the sweetness of his love."

"Well, every evening when the darkness wraps itself round my prayer, He, God, is there, disguised as a poor man watching me. When I endure, in the darkness of faith, the prolonged wait for the God who comes, He has already come to me and is embracing me silently, with the same embrace with which I, in faith, embrace Him."

The God Who Comes – by Carlo Carretto, as published in
A Guide to Prayer for Ministers and Other Servants
The Upper Room, Nashville, Tennessee. 1983

EPILOGUE

In case you are wondering how my holding patterns turned out:

- I was elected student body president in my senior year of high school.

- I married at age 26 to the perfect wife for me. And the woman I proposed to, who said she would never marry a minister, wound up doing so four years later.

- After losing a child and considering adoption, we had two children and two grandchildren.

- The 13 years in Campus ministry proved foundational and preparatory to the pastorate.

- The most challenging assignment required 11 years to complete. Thus, God and my wife did not acquiesce to my desire to quit and run away from it.

- After 21 years, my Parkinson's Disease has progressed incrementally without side effects from the medication, allowing me to function normally without drastically changing my lifestyle.

- Our children are educational professionals. Our family has a common faith, serves in people-helping professions, and we enjoy the closeness and open communication with each other and our precious grandchildren.

- Being published came in the eighth decade of my life for reasons only God knows and will someday explain to me.

Applause for Roland Boyce's previous book,
The Ultimate Calling
(*The Perils and Privileges of the Pastorate*)

It is truly an incredible work.
Craig Rush, Pastor- West Virginia

After reading *The Ultimate Calling,* my reaction was WOW. It is the most comprehensive book on pastoral call and ministry I have read, by a lot!
Bill Anthes, Pastor - New York

I love your book. It should be required reading for every seminary student.
David Lindfors, Pastor - Illinois

You have many years of wisdom and teaching this work which is of much value. What I read in the book is what I've seen in you.
Dr. Ron Marrs, Pastor/Professor – Oregon

Do yourself a favor and give yourself the gift of his insights.
Dr. Art Greco, Pastor - California

Made in the USA
Monee, IL
07 October 2023

44128517R00139